DRESS YOUR BEST

DRESS YOUR BEST

The new way of analysing your figure and your wardrobe to suit you

JANE PROCTER

Macdonald

CONTENTS

A Macdonald Book

© 1984 Marshall Editions Limited

First published in Great Britain in 1985
by Macdonald & Co (Publishers) Ltd
London & Sydney

A member of BPCC plc

British Library Cataloguing in Publication Data
Procter, Jane
  Dress your best.
  1. Clothing and dress
  I. Title
  646'.34   TX340
  ISBN 0-356-10519-9

Filmset by MS Filmsetting Ltd, Frome, Somerset
Origination by Adroit Photo Litho Ltd
Birmingham
Printed and bound in Belgium by Brepols SA

Macdonald & Co (Publishers) Ltd
Maxwell House
74 Worship Street
London
EC2A 2EN

Conceived, edited and designed by
Marshall Editions Limited
71 Eccleston Square
London SW1V 1PJ

EDITOR	Carole McGlynn
ART DIRECTOR	John Bigg
ART EDITOR	Daphne Mattingly
PICTURE EDITOR	Zilda Tandy
EDITORIAL ASSISTANT	Clare Badham
DESIGN ASSISTANT	Barbara Clarke
PRODUCTION	Janice Storr
CARE AND REPAIR	Sue Locke
ILLUSTRATORS	Lucy Su
	Shari Peacock
BEAUTY EDITOR	Rosemary Mills
	Company Magazine

LONDON NEW YORK ©

Jeeves International

CONSULTANTS FOR CLOTHES CARE

As the author of *Dress Your Best*, I think it's only fair that I should let you into a few secrets. When I'm getting dressed in the morning I often change my clothes three or four times until I hit on an outfit that feels right. I agonize over every item I buy and I panic each time I'm invited to a dressy occasion. Added to that I'm seriously quite busty and my clothes budget is far from vast.

But I have an unerring belief that I'm not alone. I came to the conclusion long ago that anyone who looks marvellous, but insists that they simply throw on the nearest thing to hand, is fibbing.

Dressing well and looking good in your clothes is hard work, whether at the planning, the buying or the wearing stage – or at all three. Admittedly some people have it easier than others. Working with a contemporary or near-perfect figure is the prime factor because, quite simply, it is easier to dress a standard shape. And with the direction that fashion has taken for the best part of this century it is also true that the slimmer (and, to complete the mis-quoting of Wallis Simpson's acute observation, the richer) you are, the less problems you are likely to have.

But very few women have model-girl figures; if you want confirmation and a good cheering-up at the same time, visit a communal changing room. Clothed, most of us look more or less all right, most of the time. This book is about looking great.

The clothes we choose can flaunt or hide our bodies. What I hope *Dress Your Best* will illustrate is not how to hide or flaunt, but how to flatter.

Getting your body into reasonably good shape is the best starting point. I say *reasonably* good shape because perfection is what marketing dreams are made of and far too depressing to contemplate in real life.

Forget the notions put about by the fitness fanatics who claim that with a bit of exercise and healthy eating anyone can achieve the body beautiful. That's nonsense. We all can and should reap the benefits of exercise and sensible diet and attain a far better body – sleek and toned, with glowing skin, sparkling eyes and shiny hair. But if you start out with, say, short legs, narrow shoulders or wide-boned hips your improved body will still have short legs, narrow shoulders or wide-boned hips. Don't blame yourself, blame your parents!

But this is where clothes come in. The joy of clothes is that nobody need know that your body wouldn't win you a modelling contract if you learn how to dress deceitfully – or, if you prefer a prettier word, intelligently. A few tricks with line and optical illusion, a clever choice of colours and a sound knowledge of how texture relates to your shape, should have everybody praising your new-found figure.

Our figures are only one element in the dressing right equation. There are many more bugbears.

Fashion itself is the main culprit – or, strictly speaking, the lack of a single fashion. Way back when, it was all so easy. Paris decreed a line and everyone who aspired to fashion followed it. And all those who didn't still approximated to the current style, albeit in a watered-down version, because everything they could find in the shops related to it.

Nowadays there is no one line, but numerous lines. We all have the freedom to select from many fashions and to wear exactly what we choose. But this very liberty is dual-edged. On one hand nobody need be forced into an outfit that is patently unflattering, but on the other hand, without a steely sense of your own taste and direction, the countless options can be merely bewildering.

The life you lead often adds complications too. Consider how many roles you play even on a fairly quiet day. It's more than possible that you play chauffeur on the school run, office manager, grocery shopper and company hostess, all without a chance to change. The clothes decision behind that act would tax a computer.

Lastly we come to the most important factor in your appearance – your personality. If you dress out of context you may feel a trifle uncomfortable, but if you dress out of temperament you'll appear ludicrous. Some people are miraculously stable – a feature that simplifies clothes buying immensely. But if like me your mood swings with the wind, don't make the mistake of pulling on your utilitarian dungarees when there's a neon sign in your head insisting that today's the day for silly frillies. Your personality is the element that makes fashion so much fun – and it's also the one which means that any book on the subject is bound to be full of contradictory notions.

You'll find that some sections of *Dress Your Best* seem tailor-made for you, while others make you groan at the severity or giggle at the frivolity of it all. I hope so – fashion is a perverse but joyous business. Don't dismiss out of hand unlikely or strange ideas; they could well be the inspiration that helps you break out of a dressing rut. But most of all don't take your clothes too seriously. If you lose sight of the wit and charm of fashion, dressing will indeed become a boring slog. But if you remain irreverent, you'll not only enjoy your wardrobe but, quite simply and quite naturally, achieve the vital ingredient – style.

Dress Your Best is designed to help you achieve style and confidence. Firstly while you are shopping, when those expensive buying decisions are made, and then every morning and evening in front of the mirror.

I hope that you enjoy reading the book, and if you discover just one new idea that makes dressing your best that little bit easier, then I will feel that it has succeeded.

Jane Procter

ANALYSE YOURSELF

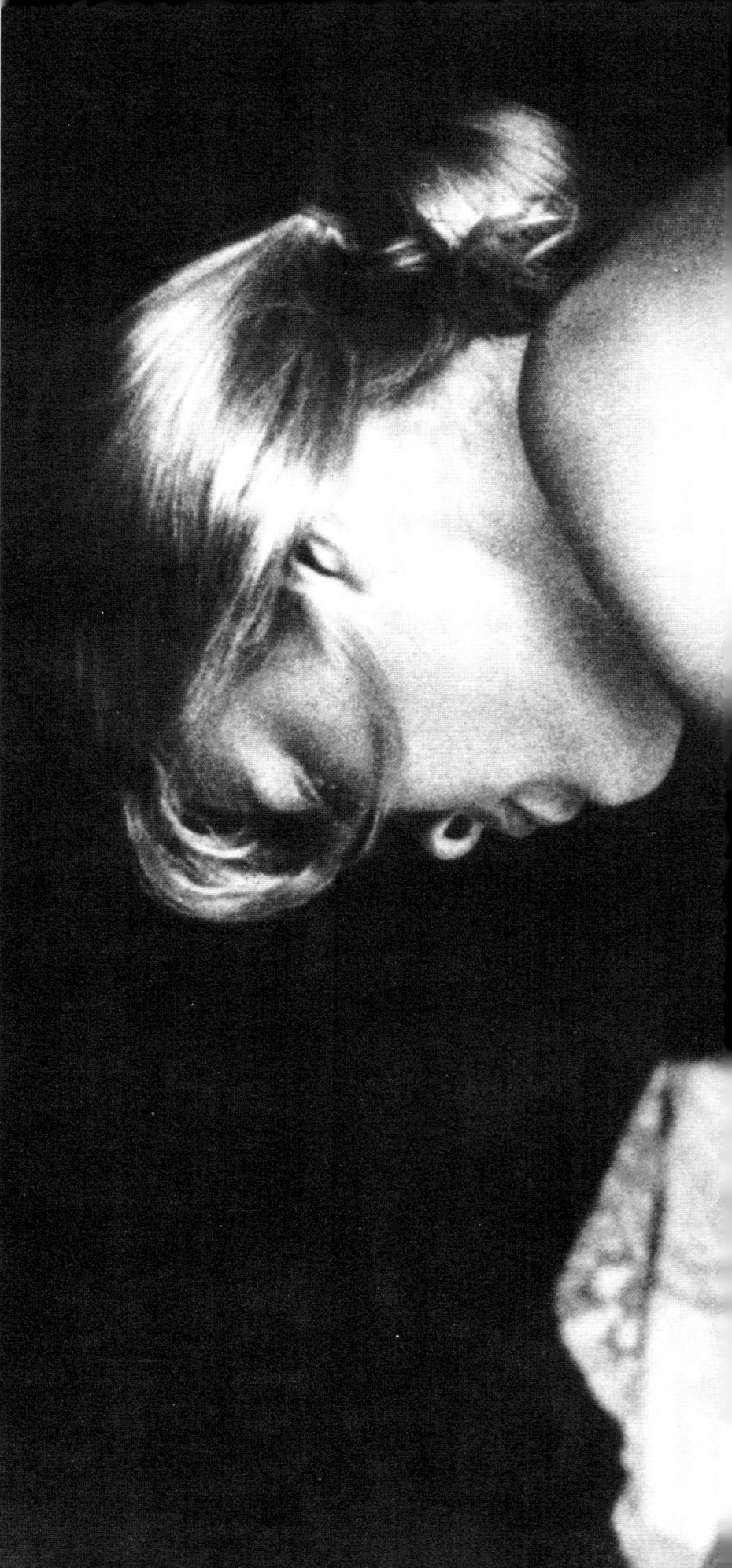

If you are unhappy with the way
you dress, consider what is letting
you down. It could be anything
from lack of confidence or a
difficult body shape to a haphazard
approach to shopping or planning,
a sprawling wardrobe or limited
finances. Use this chapter to come
to terms with your shape, your
lifestyle, your budget. Once you
know yourself better, you're well
on the way to a more confident
and individual way of dressing.

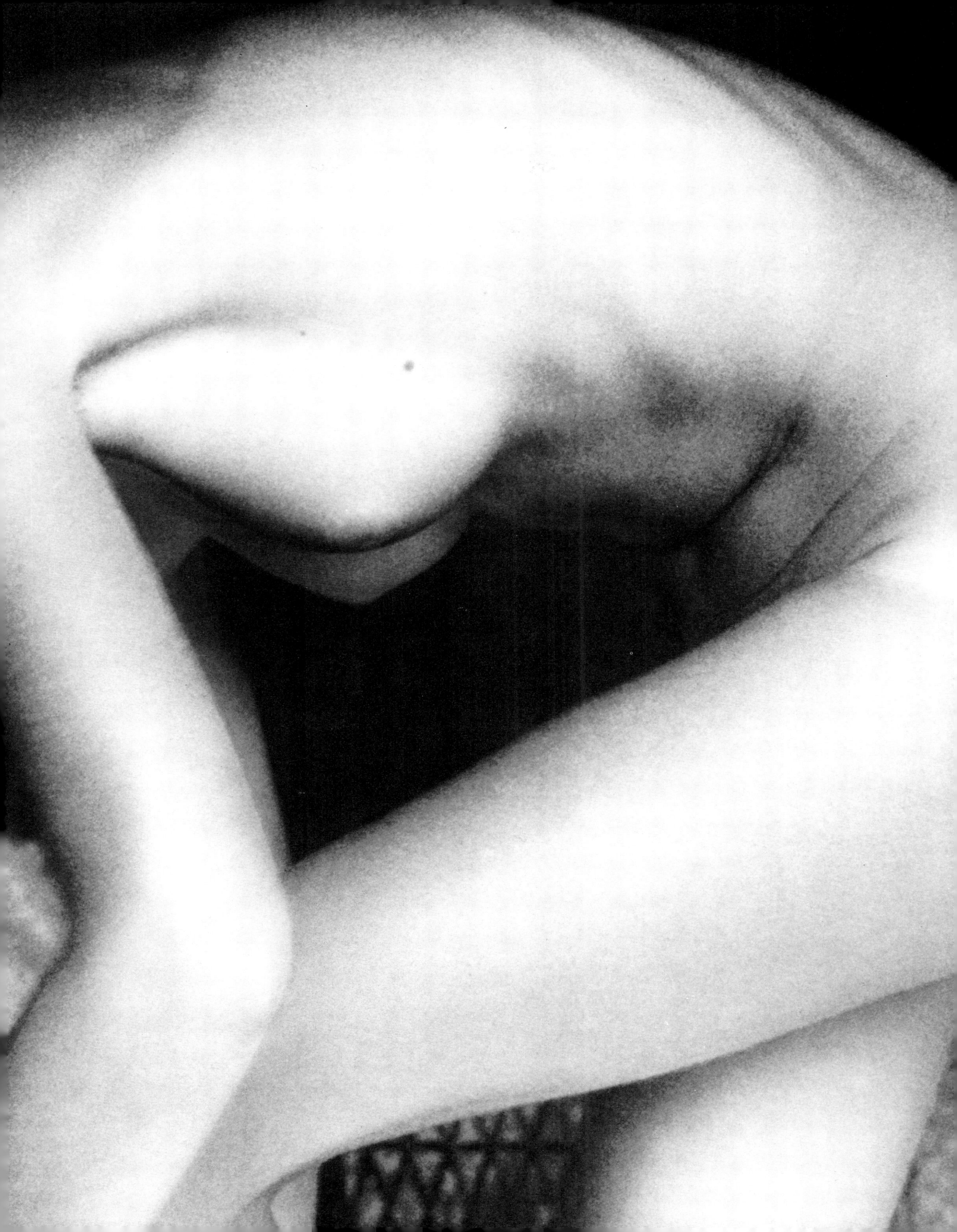

Our clothes are the first impression we give the world. What we wear is as basic a form of communication as the spoken language – it may indicate our background, age, occupation, politics and sense of humour. But there's absolutely nothing wrong with using wardrobe tactics to successfully project the image you choose.

WHO ARE YOU DRESSING FOR?

What you choose to wear depends on so many factors. Consider firstly who you dress to please – is it yourself, your boyfriend or husband, your family, girlfriends or work colleagues? Do you identify, for instance, with a particular peer group and thus adopt the uniform of the set?

Some women are in a quandary where clothes are concerned. They either haven't decided quite who they are (or what image they wish to project), or they haven't mastered the art of dressing true to their personalities. They constantly confuse people with the conflict of signals they send out. Your choice of fashion must reflect your *own* character – it can change, but then so too can your character. It's never a good idea to be unduly influenced by a stronger personality, say that of your mother or a close friend. It only hampers relationships if the language of your clothes is out of tune with your speech. It is as disconcerting as seeing a timid girl in a see-through blouse or a tomboy in frills.

WHAT SHAPE ARE YOU?

The next requirement of establishing your own style is a thorough understanding of your body shape. This book will help you to find out what suits it best and what tricks you can play with illusion or line. You need to recognize which styles, fabrics, colours and shapes are your friends, which are your enemies. You also need to know how to disguise your weak points and to flatter and make the most of your best ones.

WHAT DO YOU DO?

Just as important as dressing for your shape is dressing in a way that's appropriate for your lifestyle, which means choosing clothes that are both suitable and practical for your job, your social life and the climate that you live in.

The pictures on this page show three women pursuing totally different activities and wearing clothes that are entirely appropriate. While these are different women, one person's lifestyle might well encompass two or even all three aspects – and several more besides. Depending on your clothes budget, this needn't necessarily mean totally diverse outfits for all the different aspects of your life. If you plan ahead and buy both clothes and accessories with care, a basic wardrobe can be transformed into the perfect backdrop for countless situations and character changes.

WHAT IS YOUR STYLE?

Establishing a way of dressing that is true to your personality goes a long way towards looking right for every occasion and never appearing under- or over-dressed. Dressing to suit the occasion – as well as to complement your shape – in clothes that are both attractive and practical is the art of dressing well. Though obvious on paper, this is rarely as simple in practice. Only a few are born with the knack of always looking right, whatever the occasion – the rest of us must work at it.

But don't be discouraged – looking good and looking 'just right' are learnable skills. Later in the book, a whole chapter is devoted to dressing to suit your individual style. This will help you to put together outfits for the many facets of your life – from business clothes to leisurewear, and from evening dress to sportswear, as well as packing for a summer holiday or a weekend in the country.

Style is individual: it's different for each person and impossible to define in general terms – what may look super-stylish on one person can appear ridiculous on another. Personal style has nothing to do with following all the latest fashion trends. It is about dressing in a way that reflects your personality and making the most of yourself – and if that happens to include the latest hot styles, that's fine – but if it doesn't, that's fine too.

In creating your own unique style, you will develop the confidence to treat fashion with a healthy and interested respect, to pick what flatters and discard what doesn't. Fashion should always be fun, so treat it irreverently and make it work for you.

THE CHAMELEON APPROACH

Most fashion manuals expect you to find a look that suits you and then stick with it. This is one approach to dressing well but it is only one of many and certainly the most limiting. It may be ideal for the woman who has to look smart but is not really interested in clothes, but it is boring for the fashionably aware and inventive dresser.

There is no great sin in being a chameleon – it may be more expensive but it's much more fun. And there are literally hundreds of fashion roles to play. As long as you don't take it all too seriously but enjoy swapping from city slicker or jolly matelot to languid lily in the space of hours, you can act as many characters as you wish – or, for that matter, can afford.

Do you have a true idea of how you look? Do you know your exact measurements? You probably have a notion of your dress, bra and shoe size but a much vaguer picture of how you really appear. How many times have you been amazed by pictures of yourself? How many excuses – cameras lie by adding inches, it was a good, or an off-day – do you conjure up?

The first step towards dressing well is a thorough understanding of your body size, its shape, its fluctuations and above all its best features. Until you get to grips with those and realize how you compare to the rough average that dress designers treat as the norm, you can't begin to cope with your body image, or learn how to play up your best points and detract from those you'd prefer to forget.

Start by measuring yourself. Your tape measure, in conjunction with a full-length mirror, is a much better guide than your scales when it comes to establishing your body image. Measure not just your bust, waist and hips but all the intricate lengths, widths and girths detailed on the diagrams below. Ask a friend to help – you will be less likely to cheat and some of the measurements are difficult to gauge accurately by yourself.

You may be wondering why you should measure your arms, for example, if you never buy anything by sleeve length. It's all to do with proportion and balance – until you know the length or circumference of your arms you probably don't know how they relate to the size of the rest of your body and how to choose the most flattering sleeves. Similarly, once you have established that you are low-waisted, you'll be better equipped to find the most successful combination of separates.

Measuring up is sure to present you with all sorts of anomalies, some cheering – a long neck or legs rarely looks amiss – and some infuriating – a short waist doesn't give exciting belts much of a stage. More important, you will ascertain how far you tally with or differ from the current 'ideal', or the standard manufacturers' size to which you are nearest. (A sizing chart is given on page 156.) But don't worry if you feel that you don't measure up. There is, mercifully, no single 'right' size for women and the average varies, not only from country to country but also across regions and in some instances across town.

And it's not just the measurements that count. Consider absolutely everything that you do or don't like about your body – from the loathed or loved freckles to your elegantly high insteps – and your attitude to them.

Some women, for example, think that generously endowed breasts are a distinct advantage and delight in flamboyant de-colletée, whereas others feel their big bust is ungainly and mars the line of the fashionably chic clothes to which they aspire. The very thin may glory in their boyishly adaptable figures or yearn for a few feminine curves. Most short girls long to add inches, but not all tall girls carry their height proudly. If you are honest about your feelings, it will become crystal clear what features need accentuating and which to play down – and this is where the right choice of clothes comes in.

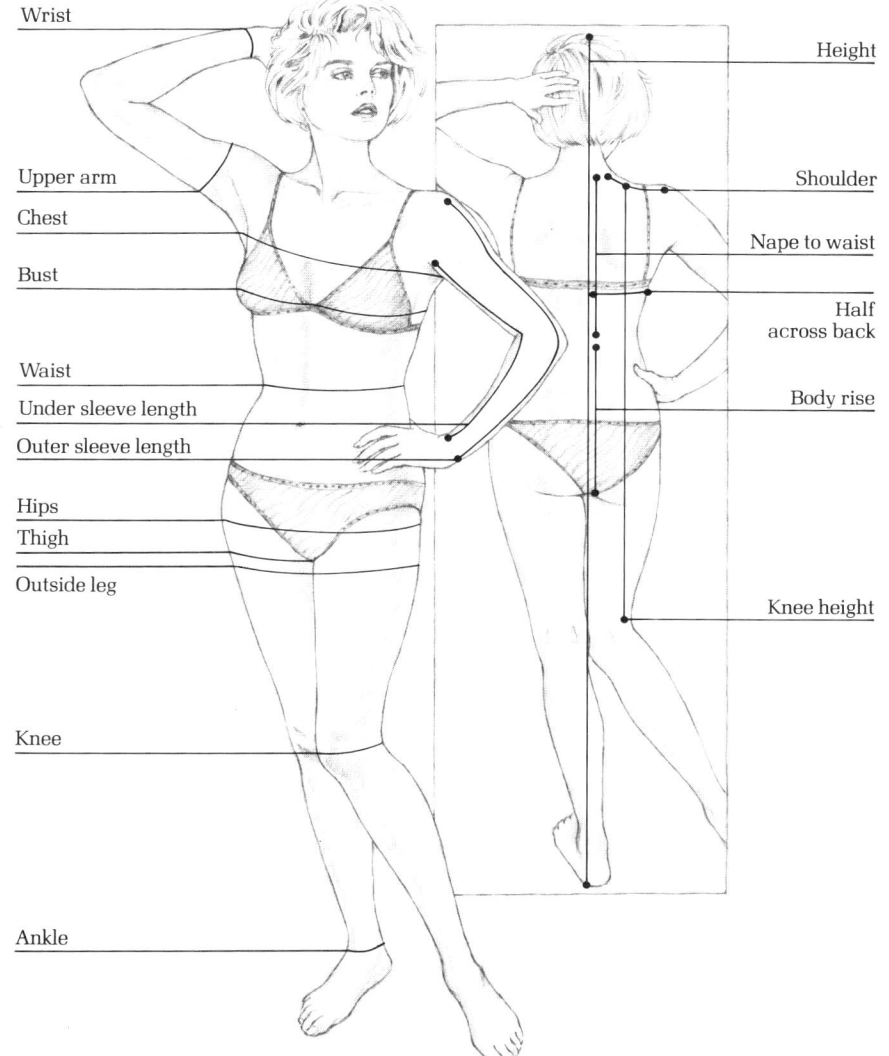

Wrist
Upper arm
Chest
Bust
Waist
Under sleeve length
Outer sleeve length
Hips
Thigh
Outside leg
Knee
Ankle

Height
Shoulder
Nape to waist
Half across back
Body rise
Knee height

Once you've taken these measurements, compare them to those in the chart on page 156. This will indicate what clothes size you should generally buy. You'll also have a better idea of the proportions of your body, which will help when it comes to choosing clothes that balance these out.

WHAT SIZE SHALL I BUY?

You may be surprised to hear that clothes do not come in standard sizes, but only approximations of them. There are guidelines set out for manufacturers to interpret which give the maximum and minimum for each vital statistic. But, as the chart on page 156 shows, these can vary up to 3in (7cm) either way, which explains why most women own garments with two or even three different size labels in them.

If you always choose the same make of clothes you have some chance of consistently buying the same size. Even then, tolerance levels in modern manufacturing techniques can allow for wide discrepancies in otherwise identical items – which explains why trying on two of the same sized garment can often yield one that is a better fit for you.

While the horizontal measurements by which we buy our clothes are very hit and miss, the vertical measurements, ie. nape to waist, or body rise, are even more arbitrary, and rarely allow for the tremendous variation of lengths that women come in. A few manufacturers and specialist shops supply petite or longer lengths, but they are in the minority, and anyway there is no rule to say that because you are long-waisted you are necessarily long-legged.

If, like men, we stuck to a two- or three-piece suit, we would find that each chest size was available in at least five different permutations of length and waist measurement – but what women would prefer the anonymity of a uniform? The simple reason for the lack of alternatives in women's clothes sizes is that with the huge range of styles available to women it would be impossible for stores to stock wide ranges of each item. If they carried sizes 8–18 it would mean stocking at least 30 different sizes of each garment.

So while it's worth knowing the standard size you're generally closest to, it's important to be open-minded and to try on a size up or a size down, depending on the make. It's always useful to know of a particular designer who cuts clothes that fit you, or indeed several – you might stick with one for skirts, another for trousers and a third for dresses.

Sweaters do not generally present a problem – as they are rarely intended to be body-hugging, their cut is less crucial. But there's really no substitute for trying clothes on – in several sizes and several styles – and studying the effect in a mirror. For some lucky shoppers, this is half the fun of buying clothes – for the rest of us it's a necessary evil if we want to dress our best.

PUMPING IRON

Over the past two decades or so, the shape of women in general has been changing. The very ideal of feminine beauty – the softly rounded fragile female form – has been replaced by a firmer, stronger, more active one. Today the look is lean, fit and athletic with no one feature or area over-emphasized.

A survey carried out, showing the difference in size of women of the same weight comparing 1951 with 1972, revealed that women have become generally taller, while the waist circumference has increased and bust and hip size has slightly decreased.

Glowing health, vitality, awareness and action are essential qualities for today's woman, who is no longer afraid to flex her muscles. The well-toned, powerful body has proved to be both fashionable and beautiful. Body builders rely a lot on isometrics, such as weight-lifting and muscle-tension exercises. Little actual movement takes place, just the tensing of muscles against machines or a wall.

For dynamic fitness, aerobics provide the answer, involving rhythmic movements of your arms and legs, putting your body under measured, steady stress. Running, jogging and dance as well as swimming, rowing and cycling are all examples of aerobic activities which require large amounts of oxygen.

It's a rare woman who is happy with her body shape and the one who thinks she is normal is virtually impossible to find. Even the pretty, seemingly well-proportioned model may be harbouring a grudge about her odd-sized feet.

But every woman has her own optimum form and it's important to keep the body you've been bestowed with in peak condition. Whether you're long, lean and angular or short, compact and sturdy, being fit is the vital factor. And as long as you follow sensible body maintenance, which includes healthy eating, enough sleep and regular exercise, you should have a body you can come to terms with.

Within limits, it's perfectly possible to re-align your body—slim it down, give it added muscles or curves, walk in a way to enhance its shape, and dress in a fashion to celebrate its beauty.

Before you can do anything with your body, you have to understand it and know exactly what you've got. Naturally there are enormous variations in frame structure and you first have to acknowledge that it's impossible to change your basic body type (see below) – so don't get a complex about what you can't alter. Knowing these basic builds exist will help you to be more realistic about your own body and to choose clothes that work for you rather than fighting your basic shape. You can learn instead to work within its possibilities.

Very few of us have a true idea of how we look. Some people never look at themselves out of their clothes and others only see their body in fragments – in a face mirror, a hand mirror and odd shop-window glimpses – and never appreciated it as a whole.

The other element that prevents people coming to terms with their body image is nostalgia. How many of us carry around a dated picture of ourselves – not necessarily in our wallets but in our heads?

The obvious starting point is to measure your body thoroughly, as indicated on the previous page. Another useful exercise is to have your photograph taken (preferably in a bikini) standing alongside a large, immutable object such as a pair of step ladders. The photograph will show how you compare to an object that you know well. It has to be a fixed size because humans relate to other people in subconscious terms of their own body size. If your weight fluctuates, a companion of stable weight will appear to increase and decrease in direct proportion.

Study the photograph to find out more about your basic shape, where you need to trim up and any posture faults. Even if you have a short neck or legs, or are more rounded than others, you can still walk tall, feel good about yourself and learn to choose clothes that enhance your best features and hide your worst figure faults.

The four figures on these pages are all non-standard and represent the most common figure fluctuations. Throughout the next chapter these four shapes are represented by a code of symbols which are used to highlight outfits that work particularly well with each figure shape. These will give you an idea of what is most flattering, what to avoid – and when you can cheat.

In choosing just four figures, I am not assuming that we all fit into these four fixed parameters. It's perfectly possible to be hippy and busty – otherwise known as the covetable hourglass – or tall and carrying a lot of weight, but as the permutations are endless, the book would be too. If you don't fit in exactly with the figure codes you can, by gleaning tips relevant to different parts of your body, find a look to suit you.

You should always bear in mind that every fashion rule is made to be broken by those with the flair and imagination to transcend the guidelines. But before you disregard the code totally, remember that to flaunt the rules you first need to have a thorough understanding of what they are.

BODY SHAPES

The contours of your body are determined by your body type, your muscle tone and your distributions of flesh and fat. While your basic body type doesn't change, your weight and shape may shift, depending on age, diet, exercise and body chemistry.

There are three basic physiological shapes. Some people fit them exactly but mostly, while belonging predominantly to one group, we are mixtures.

Ectomorph Once the fashionable ideal, she is thin, without much muscle or fat but with some bust shaping. She has a small frame with narrow shoulders and often narrower hips than shoulders.

Mesomorph The current favourite shape is medium build, with a lot of muscle and bone but not much fat – though she can thicken up with lack of exercise. The frame is medium to large, ranging from athletic to rounded. Sometimes broad-shouldered and a forceful shape, but with a degree of narrowness through ribcage, waist and hips.

Endomorph A heavy build, rounded on all sides with a chunky middle section – though not necessarily a large frame. Well-covered, but without excess fat, and with firm muscles, her shoulders are often narrower than her hips.

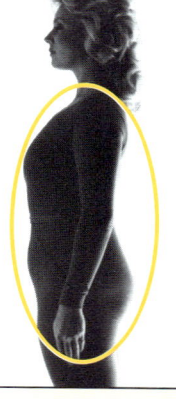

Rounded all over – a bit too much of a good thing. First consider losing a few pounds, because apart from the surplus you're probably in great proportion. But if losing weight is too daunting, just remember never to wear anything tight, and don't display too much flesh.

Straight up-and-down – most people would assume you had no grouse about your figure. Reed slim, you make the perfect coat hanger. But you don't want to be a tomboy for ever. Use tricks of line, tucks, pleats and pattern to give you curves you've only dreamed of.

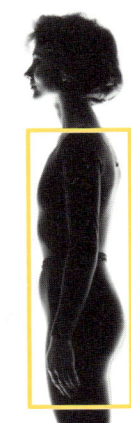

Pear-shaped – broad in the beam. You may not relish it, but count your blessings because this is the easiest figure fault to minimize. It is also the simplest shape to dress, mainly because it's the most common.

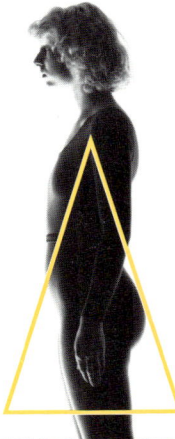

Top-heavy – the big-busted have all the pluses and most of the minuses. Yours is by far the most difficult shape to dress. Perhaps because most top fashion designers are men, the breasts are largely ignored. But don't despair – yours is also most men's ultimate fantasy figure shape.

Every woman thinks that she's the only one with problems. She assumes that anyone who is glamorous and in the public eye is sure to have a perfect body shape. But she is wrong. Celebrities are not all model-girl-shaped and, to prove it, six of the more honest and open of our famous faces – or famous names – reveal here that their figures don't quite match up with the so-called norm. But not one of them is complaining. They've all learnt, not only to live with any imperfections, but to turn them into positive plus points.

One fascinating fact emerged. It doesn't matter whether you're smaller, shorter, taller, flatter, bigger or bustier than average, shoulder pads are your best friend. All six of our celebrities agreed that they're the greatest figure-flatterer, whatever your shape.

JOANNE BROGDEN
Professor of Fashion at the Royal College of Art, London.

6 Shape, whether it's in clothes, cars or furniture, is terribly important to me. If I don't have to be concerned about my shape I'm far more relaxed and more fun to be with. Since I've grown heavier, I have decided always to wear a jacket or overshirt. And nowadays I never take my jacket off. 9

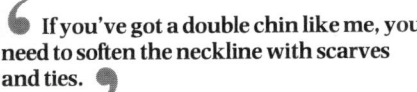
❝ If you've got a double chin like me, you need to soften the neckline with scarves and ties. ❞

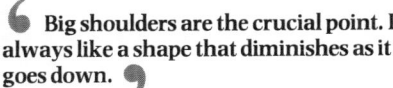
❝ Big shoulders are the crucial point. I always like a shape that diminishes as it goes down. ❞

❝ I vary my heel heights to balance outfits. On me a dress demands a higher heel. ❞

❝ I prefer wearing trousers to skirts, as long as I can wear a big shirt or jacket over the top. The basic quality is a tunic look. It's not the ease of trousers that appeals, but the silhouette. ❞

ANALYSE YOURSELF

TOYAH WILCOX
'Toyah' successfully combines two careers, as a rock star and an actress.

6 I may only be 4 feet 11 inches, but I don't feel small. I wear black and bold red to give me presence and height. I don't like to show off my legs as they're the shortest part of me. 9

6 Built-up shoulders are great, especially the Samurai-style, where the shoulders are cut to jut out. They not only flatter the hips, but give the impression of a firm, muscular physique – and a taller one. 9

GERALDINE JAMES
Actress whose starring roles include that of Sarah Layton in the television serial, *The Jewel in the Crown*.

6 Tight skirts, narrow-bottomed dresses and jeans are all fine when slim – but with a tendency to put on weight easily it's a very short way to go before I bear a startling resemblance to the back of a bus. 9

6 Broad shoulders can be wonderful – shoulder pads make it look as though they're meant to be there. But I have a broad back and a big bust as well, which makes things difficult. 9

6 Skimpy T-shirts, shorts, square tops, bright patterns and pale colours can all be dangerous. I avoid them unless they can be covered by a long, loose jacket. This is my favourite single item of clothing and I have dozens. 9

CAROLYN SEAWARD

Actress, famous for her role as a 'Bond girl' in one of the James Bond films.

❛ I wear a size 34D bra and I'm proud of it. You have to have a bust to wear certain clothes – a boned bodice like this would look stupid on a flat chest. And in a dress like this a big bust does make your waist look smaller. ❜

❛ I never wear loose, baggy jumpers as they make me look frumpy and big all over. I add shoulder pads to sweaters to give a stronger, slimming line. ❜

Carolyn Seaward

MARY PARKINSON

Television presenter and wife of Michael Parkinson, famous television chat-show host.

❛ I'm skinny, flat-chested and rather bony, but at 5 feet 8 inches and only a size 12 it can be an asset to be straight up and down. Wrongly dressed, I can look hard and angular, so I have to choose clothes that envelop me and soften the hard edges rather than bare all. A slip of nothing will do just that and with sweaters, for instance, anything clingy is right out. There has to be a lot of sweater so that what there is of me can look good underneath. ❜

❛ Shoulder pads are wonderful for a figure like mine because they manage to give it shape. ❜

❛ Backless is perfect for me; it makes people forget that I've got no front. ❜

Mary Parkinson

VICTORIA PRINCIPAL

Actress made famous by her role in *Dallas*, and author of *The Body Principle*, a book of exercises designed for fitness.

❛ My bust and I have been together so long, I've learned to cope with it. Short jackets are completely out of the question for me as, once they have skimmed over my bust, they continue sticking out. ❜

❛ Slim, tailored jackets must be padded on the shoulders to balance my bust. I like my clothes to start broad at the top and gradually taper to the knee. ❜

❛ There are lots of things I have to avoid. I've got small bones and I'm busty. I never buy big patterns or high waists and I avoid decolletée. I prefer to give just a hint of what's beneath rather than expose it. ❜

ANALYSE YOURSELF

The ultimate route to a well-planned wardrobe would be a robbery. If all your clothes were stolen and you were forced to start again with only limited compensation from an insurance company, you could then aspire to the ideal capsule wardrobe.

Drastic steps apart, collecting a group of clothes that work well together and cater for all occasions *is* possible, even with the clutter that we all accumulate along the way.

Flexibility is the key. A wardrobe made up of versatile separates will go anywhere, any time with anyone. Pared down to the essentials, your basics should fit into a regular suitcase and cover all eventualities indefinitely. This demands keen planning and eliminates all but the occasional impulse purchase.

To get the most out of classic separates you must understand the techniques of wardrobe stretching. Mix and match is the starting point, added to the discipline of never buying anything with limited use, that suits only one or two occasions or can be worn with only one other thing.

Beautiful basics like blazers, trenchcoats, pleated skirts and hacking jackets are at home in almost any wardrobe and make the perfect backdrop for the personal stamp. The stylish woman can add her own flair with a selection of the collectibles – the items you can never have too many of – like cashmere sweaters and mufflers, silk and cotton shirts, leather belts and kid gloves.

The safest way to collect the basic ingredients of your wardrobe is to stick to a strict colour scheme. Monochrome is the easiest and the most extreme example of this. If you own only black and white you can reach into your cupboard blindfold and be almost sure of perfect partnerships.

Most of us suffer at some time or another from the panic of 'I haven't a thing to wear' – even when faced with a full wardrobe. Again, this is where planning comes in. We all tend to stock up on the clothes we find easiest to buy – which, naturally, are the ones we like wearing most. Consequently we never reserve enough hunting time or money for the real gaps in our wardrobes.

It takes discipline and imagination to buy or adapt our clothes for every eventuality. A useful exercise is to go through last year's diary and pick out all the occasions for which you had trouble finding the right things to wear (for me it's dressy evening do's). If you don't already own it you must find it difficult to shop for, but then at least you will know what you should be looking for.

PERSONAL STYLE

Consider how and why you buy your clothes. Do you copy slavishly from fashion magazines? Do you try and emulate an admired television or movie personality or even a particular friend or colleague, by searching out similar garments to reconstruct their style? Or do you consider your own lifestyle – your job, your friends, your hobbies – as well as your shape, colouring and taste, and then decide logically what you need and what will look right on you?

A mixture of all three approaches will probably work best. This may seem a surprising route to achieving an original but coherent style, but too much logic can be dull and carbon-copy dressing will dominate your personality. It doesn't really matter where you get your inspiration from as long as the end result works successfully.

It is essential to invest in clothes that really matter to you, that make sense in your life. If you are happiest in skirts, there is no rule to say you should ever wear trousers, except possibly for sporting activities. And the reverse applies except at some grand social occasions or in exclusive restaurants and clubs. It is important to feel comfortable and to be yourself, not a victim of the current vogue.

True style owes a lot to organization and knowing exactly what you own, so that you can add the 'vital' new pieces from season to season. Pack away specialist or very hot or cool clothes to give maximum seasonal visibility in your closet. A well-planned wardrobe never lets you down – discipline now will save anguish in the long run.

A clear and visible method of storing clothes is vital. If something is hidden away, it's too easy to forget that you own it.

Without a full-length mirror how can you tell if the proportions of an outfit work and what shoes go best with it?

Keep hats in hat boxes or at least in dust-free areas.

Never hang sweaters or knitted dresses, they will stretch out of shape. Fold them in a pile, the heaviest at the bottom.

Scented drawer liners and sachets will sweeten your clothes, especially welcome if your chest of drawers or wardrobe is old or antique.

Put dirty or badly creased clothes straight into the laundry basket. Everything in your wardrobe should be clean, pressed and ready to run.

- The key to all wardrobe mixing is proportion – but remember that the ideals change. When you discover a fresh combination, check that the balance is contemporary.

- Coordinated separates in the same colour are one thing. Learn to team together toning items to stretch your wardrobe still farther.

- Impulse buys: a dress bought on the spur of the moment may be a huge success, but when it comes to integral pieces, think about how the new item will relate to the rest of your wardrobe.

- If you make an expensive mistake, you don't have to live with it. It may be perfect for someone else, so try selling it.

THE INFLUENCE OF FASHION

How important is high fashion to you? By dint of its short life, it passes most of us by and its tricks and nuances can be so temporary that only the dedicated stylist would presume to attempt them. However, we can all use accessories to add a contemporary flavour and, far more crucial, be on the look-out for innovative shapes that will become our wardrobe staples.

Try and spot what will become a lasting fashion trend without getting too caught up in the fads that proliferate every season. Lasting trends come in slowly, peak and then gradually disappear – witness Japanese-inspired loose clothes – while fads are an overnight sensation. Don't worry if an incoming fashion trend is hard to accept at first – it's all a question of getting your eye in. A year later it will seem comfortably familiar but it's more exciting if you can be bold enough to take it up at the beginning.

Never forget that fashion should be fun, and short-lived ideas can be the most amusing of all. But unless your budget is endless, make the one-minute wonders cheap, chuck-away buys, not overdraft items.

If you do own something fashionable but not over-gimmicky, don't throw it out at the end of the season. Fashion goes in cycles and as long as there is plenty of wear left in the fabric, it may come into its own years from now. Pack it in tissue and store it in a dry place. If you keep an inventory of what you pack away you can easily pull something out and resuscitate it. You may have to change some details like the buttons: fashion has an evil knack of never cropping up exactly the same.

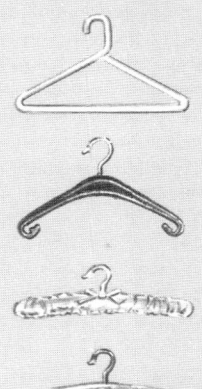

ALL HUNG UP

The ideal wardrobe would have space to hang almost everything but with limited hanging space, make room for coats, jackets, skirts, dresses and trousers. Divide up suits, so that it's easier to work out the possible permutations.

Never use wire coat hangers. Wooden or padded hangers will stop ugly crease marks around the shoulders of dresses and jackets. Hang trousers from press hangers to prevent fold marks.

Store tights rolled, either in a drawer or in a compartmentalized hanger. If you have room, hang scarves over hangers – you're sure to use them more if they catch your eye when dressing.

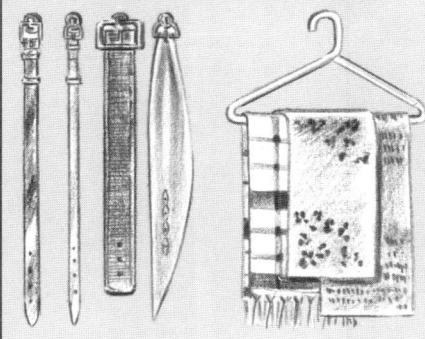

SHOE CARE

Treat shoes and boots with respect. The cost of shoe and boot trees pays dividends in lengthening the life of your footwear.

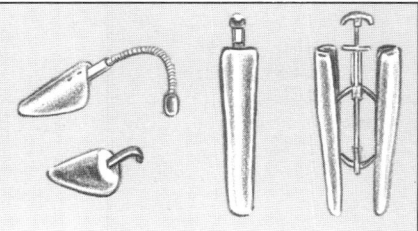

21

Fashion can be an addiction and, once hooked, we all crave a purchase fix from time to time. Sticking to a limited clothes budget can be a bit miserable for all of us – but it can also lead to inspiration in the way we dress. A tight budget teaches us to put our needs into perspective and to discipline our spending in order to make sure that every item we buy pays its way. This discipline helps us keep to a consistent style and, more importantly, it forces us to rely on our own creativity. The fashion-conscious woman does not need the crutch of expensive, designer clothes to create her own unique look.

One way of dressing on limited means is to stick with inexpensive chain-store buys which can then be imaginatively accessorized – but it is certainly not the most inspired. More interesting and extreme approaches are categorized by the expressions 'investment dressing', favoured by the classically minded, and 'rummage and revive' for the eccentrics who thrive on market stalls, army surplus and thrift shops.

Investment dressing is summed up by the catchphrase 'cost per wear' which was coined by Ingeborg Day in the American style manual *Cheap Chic*. The theory is simple: the cost of an item divided by the number of times it is worn equals the cost per wear. It is a way of comparing the value of different clothes in terms of quality and in the context of your own lifestyle. In literal terms it means that a coat costing £100 that is worn a hundred times works out at just £1 a wear, whereas the sales day bargain that set you back only £50, that you tire of quickly and only wear four or five times, costs you £10 an airing.

To most people's minds investment dressing is another way of saying classic or safe dressing. The recognized ingredients – blazers, hacking jackets, coordinating suits, tailored shirts and mid-heel court shoes – may appear to be one and the same, and obviously are so for the woman who loves the security of elegant basics. But these sort of investments can be an expensive waste for others. If your style is boiler suits and bandannas, then those are your investment clothes, not twinsets and straight skirts.

Clothes should always make us feel good rather than sensible, so we must choose clothes that we love and long to own – they are the ones that will suit us and give us a special individual style.

However outstanding an individual item, make sure that the price of a single piece won't stretch your budget so far that you won't be able to afford enough other clothes. And don't invest in clothes that you can't afford to keep up. Expensive dry cleaning bills can cripple limited finances.

With classic clothes you must be prepared to make a considerable initial investment. Then you can rely on their 'cost per wear' to pay dividends. It is sad but true that with elegant, tailored clothes, something that is expensive is not necessarily good, but an item that is good is bound to be expensive – like this timeless tweed suit by Margaret Howell.

SALES STRATEGY

Beware of sales. It's all too easy to make expensive mistakes. With a mark-down sale, ask yourself why an item has been reduced. All too often it is because no one wanted it, which could mean you won't either. With special purchase bargains, make up your mind if you really want something that is faulty or of inferior quality. If it is cheap and jokey, you might, but nine times out of ten you won't need it.

The only real sales bargains are in the classics department. Hunt out stock clearances of quality scarves and sweaters (in silk and cashmere if possible), timeless trousers, basic trenchcoats and good luggage. Stock up on basic items like tights, underwear and investment leather bags. Avoid anything that smacks of the latest fads. If the buyers have decided to off-load it, it's likely the trend is coming to an end.

- Invest in clothes that really count for you. Spend a lot on a suit or day dress and hunt out inexpensive evening wear, or if your priorities are opposite, reverse your buying.

- The cut of cheap clothes is often rather skimpy, so go for a larger size which will hang better.

- Treat all your clothes with equal respect, whatever they cost. Obey laundry instructions and learn how to iron well. A crisp white shirt is a crisp white shirt whether it cost £5 or £50.

- Consider your close friends' wardrobes. If, say, a ball gown is simply beyond your budget, you may be able to borrow, and lend something else in return.

Army surplus stores give you the chance to boast not how much, but how little you paid for something. But it takes know-how – and expertise with a needle – to dress with panache for peanuts. Don't eliminate the value of one special, more costly item to pull the whole look together.

All drill and no wit makes for a drab outfit, but feminine touches – a lacy scarf and gloves – lift surplus out of stereotype.

Forsake regular jewellery and the regular army for the commander's medals.

A pith helmet may verge on caricature; judge carefully if you can carry it off.

Beg, borrow or buy a chunky webbing belt to cinch in your outsized jacket.

A brass-buttoned bush jacket costs you next to nothing and comes in superior fabric with a quality finish. Why buy an inferior fashion copy?

If you wear military kit from head to toe, you run the risk of looking as though you've joined up. Team your surplus separates with elegant and lady-like culottes.

Keep sandals flat and socks rolled down, ready for action.

23

ANALYSE YOURSELF

How you wear your clothes is every bit as important as what you wear. The first thing you notice when a woman walks into a room is her carriage – how she holds herself. The woman who walks well, who stands tall and looks straight ahead appears poised and confident. Whatever figure faults she may have are minimized and her clothes hang well. The woman who slumps looks dejected and lumpy and her clothes never have the chance of looking anything but a mess.

There is no secret to walking well. It's all a question of standing up straight: ears over shoulders, shoulders over hips and hips over ankles. Check your posture with a simple test. Hang a piece of string from the centre top of a full-length mirror, then stand sideways and examine your profile. The string should cut you through the middle in neat halves. If you bulge out dramatically on either or both sides, your posture needs re-aligning.

Standing badly will not only wreck the chances of even your best clothes looking good, but will also cause painful physical problems. The most important area to watch is between the shoulder blades, because as soon as this area collapses you are forced to bend your neck in order to lift your chin.

Dreas Reyneke, a leading Physical Therapist who helps, among others, professional dancers and actors to shape up, blames most bad posture on the design of modern chairs.

' People sit much too far down the spine on soft chairs. This throws the head forward and leads to humps even in very young people. '

Standing too erect with your shoulders thrust back can cause as many problems as slumping. It produces tension and strain in the knees and back muscles and distorts the chest, which causes fitting problems.

If you are overweight you may have particular problems with posture. Excess weight strains the muscles and allows sag in the chest, stomach and bottom areas, which inevitably leads to slumping. Because of your bulk you must work harder to stand up straight. Remember to walk with a purpose and take special care of your feet. Flat feet is a condition often exaggerated by excess poundage, but whatever your size, if you have flat feet you'll never walk with a spring in your step.

If you feel comfortable in your clothes walking well should come naturally. Certain styles demand a particular movement. The strides, for instance, that you take in your trousers would be clumsy in a slim skirt and the soft swing that looks so graceful in a flowing skirt would appear stagey in a tighter-fitting garment.

If you wear high heels, make sure you know how to – and practising is the only way to get it right. Bear in mind, once you've achieved the knack, that if you constantly wear high heels you will never be able to wear low ones. High heels can shorten and deform the ham strings in your calves so it is vital to alternate heel heights in order to make sure that your legs work comfortably in all positions.

● One of the simplest ways to improve your posture is to imagine that you are a puppet with a string going up from the top of your head. This string pulling your head upwards should help you to keep your body in a straight line.

● Use no or at most one pillow. Sleeping on two pillows throws your head forward and encourages a hump.

● To hold the stomach in, tilt the pelvis forward slightly.

● If you feel that your posture needs improving, check out the Alexander Principle classes in your area. They will soon have you walking tall and proud and incidentally cure or alleviate numerous other physical problems.

CHANGING ROOM TACTICS
Never buy any clothes without trying them on (except of course from chain stores that will readily exchange). Sizing can be a very hit and miss affair: it is rarely consistent and few manufacturers' sizes are compatible. A general rule with sizing is that the more expensive the garment, the smaller the size you will need (which has not a little to do with flattering wealthy clients).

Cut also varies tremendously, not only from country to country (a notable example is French trousers) but also from designer to designer. Jasper Conran always gives his clothes a generous hip and bottom allowance because he started off his fashion-design career making clothes for his mother Shirley Conran. She does not, he admits somewhat indiscreetly, have the smallest derrière in the world.

When you try something on, scrutinize yourself from all angles. If the changing room has only one mirror use a hand mirror to get a clear view of the overall look.

Think hard about where the clothes will be worn and what they are going to have to do. Will they sit well without creasing or crumpling? Can you drive, type, run, dance, climb in and out of cars in them? To test this out, stride around in them, stretch your arms, and decide if any constriction like a fashionably tight skirt works within your lifestyle. Check the back and make sure that your exit is as good as your entrance.

If you are shopping for something that has to match up with existing clothes in your wardrobe, don't rely on your ability to carry colour in your head. Very few of us can remember a colour exactly, especially in the red and pink shades, but a belt, thread, button or trimming should not load you down too much on your shopping expedition. If you can't find a perfect match, don't compromise. Look for something that tones well rather than coordinates badly. Always check colour in both natural and artificial light.

Suitable underwear will help you to buy successfully, so either wear it or carry it with you. If you want to buy a backless dress a backless bra will be vital to all but the flattest-chested. Waist-high panties will give a flawless guide when buying trousers, and a slip will show if a sweater dress is capable of falling well.

If you are shopping for separates, wear the type of shirt, skirt or trousers that you will team with your new purchase. Getting the proportions right is the key to successful separates dressing. The correct type of shoe is always a great help too. Wearing sneakers when you are buying a long dress will only distort the impression.

Shopping in a rush invariably results in a compromise which often equals an expensive mistake. But an impulse buy, on the other hand, can be a winner. If you see something that shrieks 'buy me', then your instincts are probably right.

If possible, avoid shopping on a Saturday. First thing on a weekday morning is the best time, as the shops are practically empty and sales assistants less harrassed.

Before you buy anything, ask yourself 'Does it fit and do I really look good in it (or just good enough?)' 'Is it really what I want (or just fashionable at the moment?)' 'Does it blend with the rest of my clothes (or does that not worry me?)'

MAKING THE MOST OF YOUR SHAPE

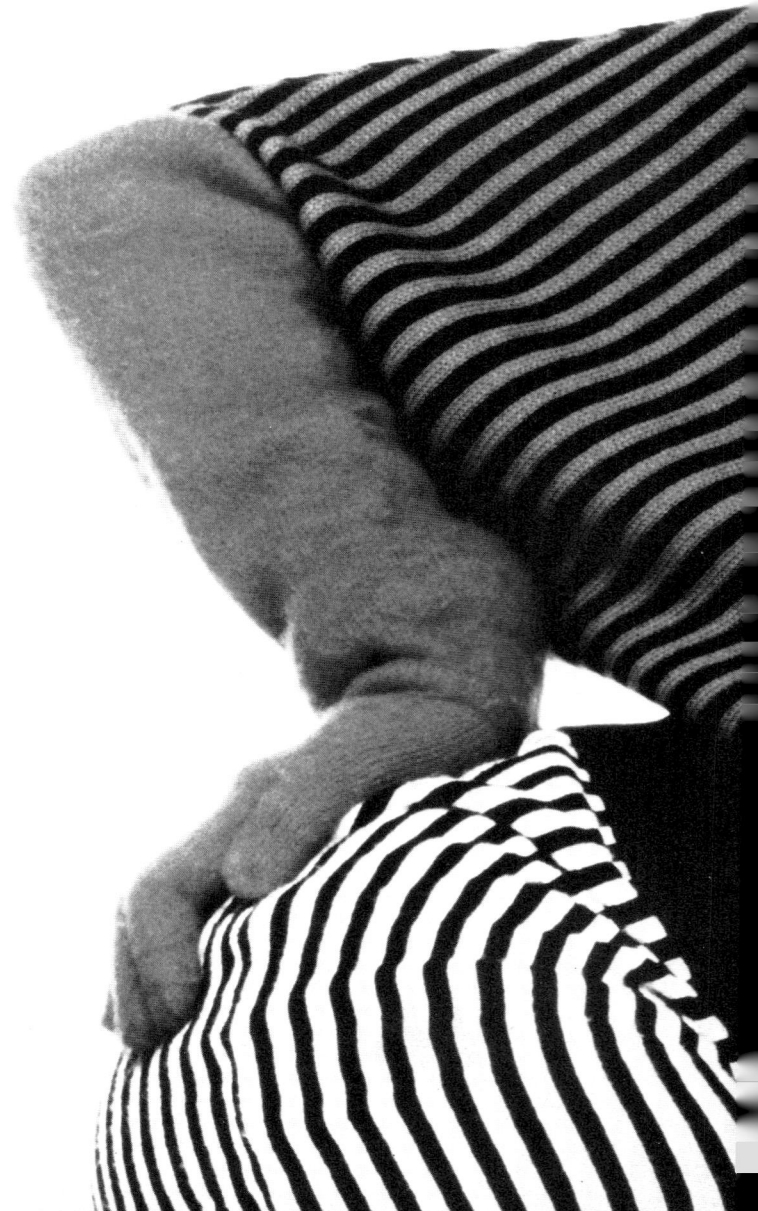

No shape is the wrong shape. It's all a matter of wearing the right clothes—the ones that flatter you. Understand the tricks of line and how to use illusion, and you can dress to suit your shape from top to toe.

There are three types of line that are relevant when it comes to choosing clothes to suit you. The first and most important is the overall outline or silhouette that an outfit creates on the body. Crucial to this is the cut of the clothes – how fitted or how full they are over different parts of the figure – as well as the neckline, the style of sleeves and the hemline.

The other two are the detail lines on a garment – the seams, joins, the type of waistline and details such as a row of buttons – and lines within the fabric itself, such as vertical or horizontal stripes. Both important in their way, these secondary lines have influences which are explored on the following pages.

Fashion is only as good as it looks on you, and today there is absolutely no reason why you should ever wear anything that doesn't suit you. Women have demanded – and got – choice in their clothes and nowadays there are at least three equally fashionable lines around at any one time.

The choice of styles found in contemporary clothes hasn't always existed. Until the 50's there was one accepted silhouette to which all fashionable women aspired, whether it suited them or not. Fashion moved slowly and for years on end a woman's shape could be totally at odds with the current vogue. As Alison Lurie says in *The Language of Clothes*, 'Women entered the second decade of the twentieth century shaped like hourglasses and came out of it like rolls of carpet.' It's clear that some women must have appeared a great deal more attractive in 1920 than in 1929 and vice versa.

Now that we have the options we must make the most of them. Looking good in clothes is all a question of proportion. If your body is built in the 'accepted' proportions of the day you will have little trouble finding ready-to-wear clothes. But if you

A feminine, faintly Edwardian silhouette mixes body hugging and body hiding.

Puffed sleeves and boat neck add definition to the shoulders and, allied to the wide, inset belt, they accentuate a neat waistline.

The fitted bodice flatters a small bust and (as long as it is not worn too tight) will not over-emphasize a big one – but a V or decorative neckline would help the top-heavy more.

Inseam pockets minimize bulk and avoid the distraction of patches.

A perfect dress for the hippy as it skirts over the widest part of the body.

Hem tucks draw the eye down.

have some non-standard feature like broad hips, buying clothes off-the-peg can become an obstacle course. It is important to realize which styles best balance and complement your figure and to know which shapes will detract from your best points.

CLOTHES SIZING

Even well-proportioned women can have difficulty finding clothes that fit perfectly, because the measurements of a standard size may vary from manufacturer to manufacturer. (A chart of manufacturers' standard measurements can be found on page 156.) And unlike men's tailored clothes, where each chest size has up to five different build variations, women's clothes tend not to allow for different shapes, or a variation of lengths, within a size.

Instead we must shop around to find designs that approximate to our given shape. It is useful to discover a particular designer who cuts clothes that fit you, as most firms are reasonably consistent with their sizing.

But finding clothes we can wear isn't too difficult these days because mass-production and the vagaries of women's sizes have had an influence on fashion which is greatly to our advantage. In the days when most clothes were run up by dressmakers, or, on a grander scale, executed by the couture houses, and when every store had a skilled seamstress on hand for minor alterations, it was possible for the fashions to be immensely fitted, with body-hugging seams. But nowadays fashionable clothes have to be much looser in cut and style. How else could they roughly fit roughly all of us?

What we now think of as a tailored jacket is invariably simply cut, and garments that do hug the figure are usually made in stretchy fabrics which achieve their snug silhouette with give, not stitches.

Lean lines make the lanky look longer, but have a slimming effect on the cuddly figure.

A dash of white adds light to the face.

A scoop neck and extended shoulderline broaden.

Break up a long arm with double sleeves, but avoid this with a big bust – the cropped sleeve adds bulk to the body's widest point.

A straight-cut tunic minimizes a big bust and gives a broad beam a slimmer silhouette.

A vertical row of buttons emphasizes the lean line.

A square boxy shape ignores the body underneath – you could be round or angular.

The slash neck and cropped sleeves complete the square impact but without the broadening effect they would have on a more fitted garment.

A sailor collar is hopeless for the top-heavy: it adds a double layer where it isn't needed.

A loose top skims over a wide waistline but can hang uncompromisingly from broad shoulders or a large bust.

Drawstring-waist trousers are great if your weight fluctuates. They also give curves to the skinny and soften the over-curvaceous.

A cropped legline cuts the leg, but now that our eyes have adapted to it we see that it reveals pretty ankles and shoes.

29

An optical illusion is something that fools the eye, making it see something that isn't really there or focus on a particular point. And it's the most useful weapon you have when it comes to dressing your best. Few of us are truly happy with our figures, but we can all use tricks with line to give the illusion of smashing bodies.

Discover what line can do for you. The eye is conditioned to move in the direction we read – left to right – and, when it sees horizontal and vertical lines of equal strength, will always relate predominantly to the horizontal. The eye also follows a straight line directly and rapidly, receiving a strong, severe message, whereas it moves slowly along a curved line and takes a softer, more relaxed signal.

When deciding on the best cut of clothes for your figure, remember that the rule is balance. If you are large take balance to the smallest point – do not, for instance, balance wide hips with wide shoulders. And if you are both busty and broad, you are best advised to use line to play down your shoulders rather than your bust.

HEADLINES
Start with your face. If it is extreme in any way – long and thin, for example, or angular – mirroring its shape in your dress or hairstyle, especially in the neckline, will only serve to emphasize it.

If you have a round face, slim it down by brushing short cropped hair forward in gently feathery wisps. Keep long hair soft to frame the face and re-shape its outline. Wearing V necklines or open collars will create the illusion of a slimmer face; they are also the most flattering for a short neck, as they visually lengthen the distance between head and shoulders.

If you have a long face, go for a heavy fringe and fullness above the ears to add balance and play up the eyes. Wear a polo or crew neck to 'shorten' your face.

Soften a square face with a mass of loose curls at the neck, or pull your hair up on top in a curly knot, pinning and fluffing it out in 40's style with lots of waving.

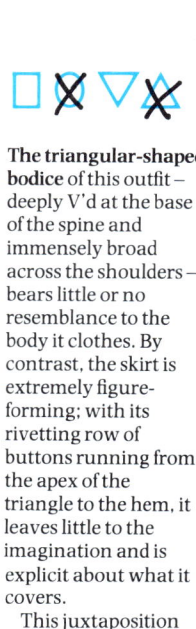

The cut of classic clothes is concerned with displaying the body's shape in the best light. But in high fashion terms cut can be employed to totally alter the body's shape for purely artistic purposes. Some designers appear to disregard the female form altogether in their pursuit of inventive and dramatic silhouettes.

The triangular-shaped bodice of this outfit – deeply V'd at the base of the spine and immensely broad across the shoulders – bears little or no resemblance to the body it clothes. By contrast, the skirt is extremely figure-forming; with its rivetting row of buttons running from the apex of the triangle to the hem, it leaves little to the imagination and is explicit about what it covers.

This juxtaposition prevents the exercise in dressing in geometric shapes from becoming a mere fashion design conceit.

SHOULDER ON

With the face as your focal point, your shoulders are next in line for attention. Clothes hang from the shoulder and its line can alter the proportion of your silhouette more than any other feature. When you shop for a shirt or a dress, look at the cut and details of the shoulderline in relation to your body.

An inset shoulder seam flatters everyone; it can be chosen discerningly to suit all shapes. If you have narrow shoulders or a large bust, an extended shoulderline will even out your proportions, and if you are broad or overweight a line seamed inside the natural shoulderline will minimize.

Any detail on the shoulders, like epaulettes, has a broadening effect. Lapels that point up will widen and those that point down will narrow. Raglan sleeves bring the line in and give the illusion of narrowing the shape, whereas an unseamed line like a kimono or a dolman displays your shoulderline and offers no pretence.

Padding emphasizes the balance, whatever your shape. Shoulder pads are the ally of both the straight-up-and-down and the over-curvaceous. On a bony figure, padded shoulders add bulk and give the illusion of curves if allied with a neat waist. When the fabric falls from big shoulders a large bust will be glossed over and a smaller waist or hips suggested.

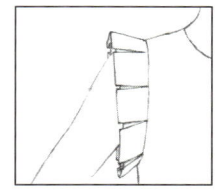

A padded shoulderline always exaggerates the silhouette. Puffed or pleated sleeves which achieve their effect with dressmaking work on the same principle as pads but in a softer and less strident way.

WAISTLINES

Waist heights, like hem lengths, are a movable feast. Use your body knowledge to ascertain what suits you best.

A dropped waistline can mean loose seaming at the hip level, a bloused effect cinching in just below the bottom or a definite froth, frill or flare.

When styles revert to the natural waistline, the length of your waist is on show. If you are short-waisted, wear a self-coloured belt or none at all. With separates, choose a belt to match your top half to lengthen the gap between bust and waist – skirts and trousers cut without waistbands are the best yet.

If you're long-waisted, go for wide belts and high-waisted designs. Cinching in a small waist will accentuate an hourglass figure, but it is often better simply alluded to with a looser belt.

The high waist emphasizes the bust, detracts from a lack of waistline and looks good on most figure shapes. It also hides a neat torso and bottom so, although not unattractive, it may hide your best points.

On the waist – by far the most natural place for it to be. If your waist is very thick don't blouse over the top in an attempt to hide it, but wear a waistcoat instead for successful camouflage.

A dropped waist can look stylish, but the top-heavy risk looking big all over if the dress falls straight from the bust in a wide line. Look for slim cuts and if necessary sash loosely just below the waist to give definition.

BLACK AND WHITE MYTHS

Some contemporary designers intend their clothes to be worn by a woman of any shape—and any age. These sweatshirting separates from young British designer Elaine Challoner illustrate the ageless feeling of form-free clothes.

One of the great myths put about by the fashion business is that black is slimming and flattering to the fuller figure. In fact it only serves to make a large body look larger. Black or any other heavy dark colour silhouettes the body against almost any background—especially the pale interiors in which most of us live. A big woman looks far prettier in calm, soft colours that trick the eye into seeing the woman not the frock. Black can, however, flatter or rather flaunt a great figure, the stark contrast detailing every curve.

The picture (left) also gives a clear example of another fashion myth being dispelled. A few years ago it would have been unthinkable to accessorize ankle-grazing skirts with flat shoes, let alone lace-up sneakers. It would have been suggested that the skirt shortens the body and demands to be balanced by some added height in the heel. Once our eyes adapt to new proportions, we find them fresh and novel—such is the ever-changing influence of fashion.

Once you understand *trompe l'oeil* tricks, you can make almost any fashion work for your body shape. The styling details on clothes and the pattern of their fabric are as significant as their cut when it comes to making the most of your figure and using the art of illusion to enhance it.

Pattern and detail—or the lack of it—are worth considering in relation to your height. If you are in proportion, your height needn't influence your choice of clothes too much. However, many short women do long to add inches. The most successful solution if you are tiny is to concentrate on vertical lines in your clothes, avoiding horizontal ones that break up the body, and to leave your clothes as uncluttered as possible.

Simple shapes which give vertical impressions, like tube or sheath dresses, will add height to a small stature, whereas exaggerated details like patch pockets, epaulettes, wide revers and very full skirts and trousers will dwarf it.

Wearing smooth fabrics, tiny prints and outfits in a single shade will all help to encourage the illusion of greater height. Choose small, scaled-down accessories and bear in mind that long straps on bags, narrow lapels, long, thin scarves, long necklaces and belts slung around the hips rather than pulling in the waist, will all visually stretch the body.

Most women regard being tall as a bonus but some lofty ladies show in the stoop of their shoulders and their hip-stuck-out stances that they'd prefer to minimize their height. The worst thing a tall girl can do is to try to hide her height with her posture. If you are tall, always stand up straight and keep your shoulders back, then choose clothes that break up long, languid lines rather than emphasize them. For instance, while a flared skirt will swirl out gracefully, a straight skirt will merely accentuate your height.

Experiment bravely with textures—bulky mohairs, tweeds, quilted fabrics and billowy satins look sensational when you've got the height to carry them off. Beware fiddly jewellery, frills and flowery hats that look fussy and keep to bold statements instead—go for big, even brash, accessories, huge, slouchy shoulder bags, splashy patterns, wide cummerbund belts and striking cuts.

When the very tall or very short girl is out of proportion, the problems are greater because her height merely emphasizes the disparity. The small girl with a full bustline or the tall girl who is carrying excess weight has to work hard in order to meld together ideas for short and top-heavy or tall and round to find her best looks.

SLIMMING STRIPES

Stripes are the most obvious form of line and far more dominant than seams or silhouette when it comes to creating an illusion.

Choose vertical lines if you want to appear taller and thinner. A single vertical is the most effective—when lines are repeated the eye moves sideways from line to line as well as up and down, and this dilutes the overall effect.

Horizontal lines emphasize width so don't ever use them on an unattractive part of the body—say, across too-large hips. However, they can be useful for evening out the proportions or for suggesting curves.

The effect of diagonal lines is dictated by their length. The shorter they are the more they work like horizontals and as they get longer they give the slimming message associated with verticals.

It might be an old chestnut, but vertical stripes really are very slimming. The girl in the leanline separates (left) certainly doesn't have measurements that most people would associate with a fashion model. She may look a little cuddly in this breezy but elegant suit, but no one would guess that she actually takes the tape at an ample 44–34–46 inches—which amounts to a statuesque size 20.

SAVING SEPARATES

Separates are a saviour for non-standard bodies. Buy them in different sizes, shapes and shades and use them to accentuate the bits you like. Always watch the join though—the eye is drawn to the point where garments meet, so don't let it be your worst.

If you're busty you can't wear anything blousy—but you can wear extraordinary trousers. Gaily printed trousers pull all the emphasis away from your bust. Wear them with something classic like a loose-fitting V-necked sweater or a tailored shirt.

Give a straight up and down figure some curves with horizontal stripes, and think yourself lucky—yours is the only shape that can get away with them.

If you are hip-heavy, don't wear a long jacket that ends at your widest point. An angular, square-cut jacket cropped to the waist, worn with the soft gathers of a dirndl skirt, is the most flattering mix of separates for your figure.

33

In 1959, it was predicted that by the 1980's underclothes would either disappear altogether or become like a second skin. In the 70's we were halfway to making this prophecy come true, what with body stockings, bra burning and naughty heroines in risqué novels running around pantie-less. But at the end of that decade, in an amazing about-turn, and in apparent contradiction of their needs or non-needs, women declared that instead of sleek, functional underwear they wanted lingerie that was sexy, pretty, glamorous and sensual.

Against all the odds, frilly and fanciful underpinnings became the desire of a great many women and beautiful garments from designers like Janet Reger and Fernando Sanchez, along with treasures found in granny's attic, fuelled the nostalgic revival. Eclipsing the lycra and polyester of modern underwear, the clamour was for silk, satin and crepe-de-Chine, real lace and embroidery, pure cotton and broderie anglaise.

Nowadays exotic lingerie has a place in almost every woman's wardrobe. Their shapes may bear little relevance to the clothes we wear much of the time. Certainly a rigid boned Basque which pulls in the waist and widens the hipline makes little sense with skinny jeans, and anything fancy, frothy or fluffy simply doesn't work with a T-shirt or slinky sweater. But sexy undies are not workaday, they are for special occasions. Wear them under a feminine frock with a proper waistline and a full skirt and you're sure to feel immensely glamorous; combine them with sober suiting and only you will know your sexy secret.

The bodice and bloomers of our great-grandmothers' era may be considered too cumbersome to wear under most of today's streamlined clothes. But worn on their own they make a deliciously cool yet provocative summer outfit.

GIRLS WILL BE GIRLS

Stockings and suspenders aren't just sexy underpinnings—as a more hygienic alternative to tights they have their sensible side too. And when it comes to waist-whittling, wearing a wide suspender belt is a great ally as it reminds you to pull your stomach in.

But however persuasive the arguments, practical or pretty, some of us simply won't put up with the lumps and bumps that suspenders cause. So if you really think tights are a turn-off, why not resort to great-granny's solution with a pair of lacy garters? But take care—if you wear them too tight, you'll stop the circulation.

GIRLS WILL BE BOYS

Silk and lacy camisoles are most girls' idea of naughty but nice undies, but others find Y-fronts for women far more appealing. Top American designer Calvin Klein started the trend for the ultimate in gender-bending with a sell-out collection of cross-dressed bodywear. With not a bra in sight, but bikini briefs, panties, singlets and boxer shorts complete with fly fronts aplenty, the range is specially adapted for female rather than male curves.

Many women are attracted to the clean lines of men's stretched cottons and the freedom of boxer shorts. Whether you choose to wear Y-fronts under frocks or to reserve the shorts for working out or jogging and the briefs for under jeans—or decide that this is a fashion you can afford to miss altogether—is entirely your affair. But judging by its success—when it was launched in New York, women ripped the designer-label Y-fronts from each other's grasp in a scrabble to snap up every shape in every shade—it's not a trend to ignore, but one with a future.

French knickers—loose-cut and elegant—win hands down on sensuality. Don't wear them under trousers, as they will ruck up and ridge. Reserve them for skirted days when you want to feel glamorous. They're good with stockings too as they cover up the bumpy bits on suspenders.

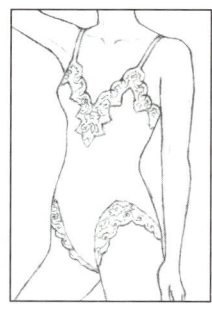

A teddy is a pared-down camiknicker. It is high-cut on the legs so that you can wear it under contoured clothes.

Wear silky camiknickers (an all-in-one combining camisole and French knickers) and you eliminate the need for bra and briefs.

A boned Basque will cinch in your waist and round out your bust and hips—it's quite the quickest way to an hourglass figure.

35

Sexy lingerie may be perfect in the boudoir, but only in rare cases is it designed to have an outer wrapping. The underwear every contemporary woman needs is the sort that gives the illusion of not being there at all.

If you don't need to wear a bra and your body is so slim that you never get a pantie ridge even under the tightest jeans, this section is not for you. But if you've ever felt that nature could do with a little improving on and that your figure needs more help than a body stocking offers, read on.

> ❛ I first got into big panties when I was modelling in Paris, for Yves Saint Laurent. He wanted the models to wear just tights under his clothes to ensure a purity of line, but I find that uncomfortable, so I compromised and rediscovered the clean lines of children's-style pants. ❜
>
> *Marie Helvin*
>
> **Marie Helvin**
> TOP MODEL

BELOW THE BELT

The best briefs are invisible. A visible pantie line is at best unflattering, at worst hideous—and it is so easy to avoid. One solution is wearing waist-high panties, another is buying them a size larger to ensure that they lie flat and smooth.

If you are a bit lumpy and the legline of your panties tends to show as well, you can cheat with a little controlling lycra from a pair of support tights. Worn under clothes, the cotton-gussetted variety (which eliminate the need to wear panties as well) will give you a sleeker line.

If you are more than a little flabby, you'll need a pantie girdle to smooth the stomach and hips. Forget the corset image—the 1980's models are made in light, comfortable fabric with subtle stretch properties. You're unaware you are wearing one, but achieve a lovely rounded, natural shape.

If you hate the thought of girdles and big panties and don't fancy the tights solution, you could go to the other extreme with a thong. A thong is the tiniest brief you could choose; it's a triangular piece of material held together with two bits of elastic, one circling the body, the other slipping between the cheeks to meet the front fabric. There's really only one unassailable rule—never wear panties without a cotton gusset. Cotton breathes and is not only more hygienic but also more comfortable.

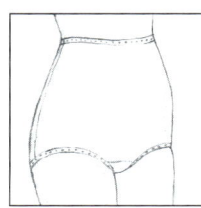

Big knickers may not be sexy—but then nor is a visible pantie line. And they do eliminate all but the worst cases of pantie ridge.

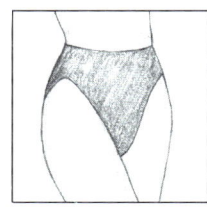

High-cut panties are excellent for the regular shaped, but aggravate pantie ridge problems for the hippy.

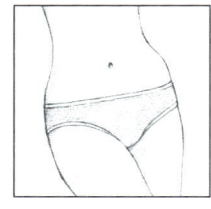

Bikini briefs are small and sweet. Wear them on the large side to prevent them cutting into your flesh.

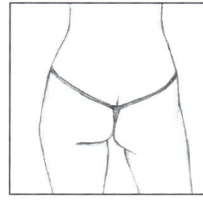

The thong is little bigger than its washing instructions and totally invisible under your clothes.

TOP SUPPORT

With a bra, the first and most important factor is fit. And if you are on the big side you are unlikely to get it right without professional advice. Never attempt to guess your size—you'd be surprised how many women wear the wrong bra size. The commonest mistake is to buy the cup too small and the band too large (for example a 38B instead of a 36C).

The time-honoured way to estimate your cup size is to subtract your ribcage measurement from your bust circumference.

---

4 in (10cm) difference is an AA cup
5 in (12.5cm) difference is an A cup
6 in (15cm) difference is a B cup
7 in (17.5cm) difference is a C cup
8 in (20cm) difference is a D cup
9 in (22.5cm) difference is a DD cup

The most reliable way is to let a trained store assistant determine your size, which she will probably do by eye. As bra sizes are rarely consistent between manufacturers, always check a new style for fit.

CHECKING FOR FIT

To put a bra on correctly, slip the straps on to your shoulders, lean forward and let your bust drop into the cups. Fasten the back, then adjust the straps. Ideally the straps should be adjusted every day to compensate for the constant subtle changes in our bodies.

When the bra is done up it should fit in a complete circle around the body and it should stay put even when you raise your arms. If it rides up at the back, it is too big.

When you try on a new bra, always make sure that there are no bulges over the top edge or at the underarm. To check for proper support, drop the straps. Support should come from the cups, not the straps, so if the whole bra sags without the straps then it's not doing its job.

- The bra is a feat of modern engineering and some contain over 50 components. Sonically welded strap joints give a stronger join than stitching.

- We all need at least three everyday bras—one to wear, one to rest and one to wash.

- Don't machine-wash, spin or tumble dry your underwear. Always dry it away from direct sunlight and don't put white undies in an airing cupboard as that will yellow them.

- Buying a bra can be compared to buying shoes—comfort and fit are essential: style is a bonus.

- A new bra should fit on the loosest hook. As it loses its elasticity with age you can use a tighter one.

- With a bigger bust, wider bra straps are necessary to avoid ridges.

- Wide-set straps are best under sundresses.

Top international model and winner of the 'most beautiful girl in the world' competition, Debi Brett is shown here wearing a moulded strapless bra by Triumph, with underwiring for firm support.

❝ I'm a size 34B so I almost always wear a bra. Underwired bras suit me best—they give the best shape and support. ❞

Debi Brett

Debi Brett
TOP MODEL

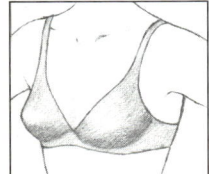

The moulded, **seamfree bra** gives the smoothest line as it is the nearest thing to a second skin.

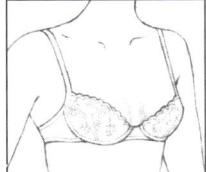

The underwired, **half-cup bra** is best on a firm bust. It emphasizes shape by pushing the bust in and up from the sides.

The underwired, **full-cup bra** is the only style that allows the busty girl to feel secure. Non-stretch straps stop bounce.

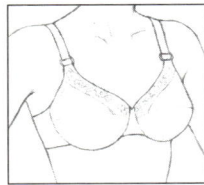

A **minimizer, underwired bra** redistributes a big bust to make it look smaller. It gives no uplift.

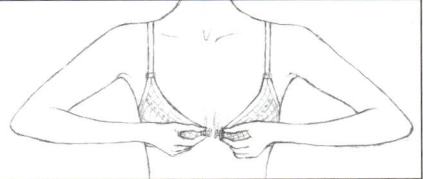

A **front-fastening bra** is favoured by some for its convenience, and is a real boon for anyone with back troubles.

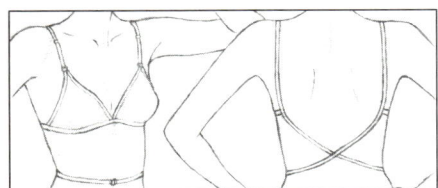

A **backless bra** makes backless fashions possible for even the fullest busted. The wrap-around straps can be attached to almost any bra or you can buy a bra which incorporates them.

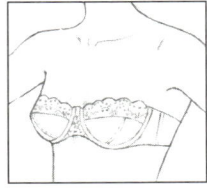

A **strapless bra** should be worn straight round the body and shouldn't be cut too low in the front.

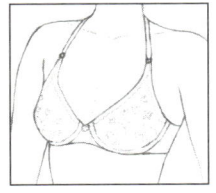

A **halter-back bra** is for wearing under halter necks or cut-away sleeve tops. It is usually better if underwired.

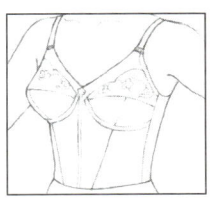

A **longline bra** smooths out midriff bulge by redistributing the flesh.

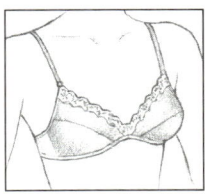

A **padded bra** augments nature to give the illusion of a larger bust. The padding under the breasts lifts the bust.

37

A brand new haircut can alter your looks drastically and is the quickest way to a new image. Don't cling to a hairstyle you've had for a long time. Just as the clothes we buy change subtly over the years, so too do the hairstyles that complement us, our clothes and our age. If you stick with a style that was right at your 'best' time, you will simply age yourself. In any case, a new cut always gives a fillip.

When choosing a hairstyle that's right for you, first consider your bone structure and the shape of your face as well as the nature of your hair. Take your lifestyle into account—there's no point choosing an elaborate style if you have no time to keep it looking its best. Ask around until you find a hairdresser who's good with your type of hair and who has style. A good rapport is essential.

The cut is the starting point, and a good cut is more important than any other single factor when it comes to the finished result. How much hair you have, its colour, thickness, straightness or curl and its rate of growth all depend on your genes. Once you realize that you have to work with what you've got, you'll have a more realistic idea of a hairstyle that flatters you. Fortunately, many of today's styles allow the hair to move, naturally and freely. However good a hairstyle you start with, it's up to you to keep it looking its best. Find the right shampoo for your type of hair, use conditioner regularly and always rinse thoroughly. Give your hair occasional deep-conditioning treatments—and don't forget it will need trimming every six to eight weeks or, in summer, even monthly.

SHORT AND BOYISH

This is a particularly good style if you have fine delicate hair which needs to be treated with the utmost care. Short, simple styles are best, as the longer fine hair is, the more easily it is damaged. Skilful cutting is important so that your hair can be left to dry naturally, avoid excessive heat during styling. The shorter and crisper the cut, the more often it needs reshaping.

Other styles to suit straight, fine hair are blunt cuts of one length, or layered cuts with quite long top layers. Wavy or curly fine hair looks best when layered.

FLUFFY AND FEATHERED

If you have medium-thick hair, you are lucky. It is usually the easiest to cope with and can be styled in a variety of ways. This layered cut encourages curly or wavy hair to curl more. Straight hair of medium thickness can also look attractive worn long and cut one length, or cut short and layered. Thin hair would also respond well to a short, layered cut to give it bounce and make it appear fuller.

The feathery ends of the hair frame the face in a soft way, while the layering gives a deliberately tousled, casual and natural effect.

In deciding the length of your hair, bear in mind a number of things. Very short, boyish hair will suit you if you have a good bone structure, big eyes and a petite figure. However, the same length hair is unlikely to flatter you if you are tall, big-boned and slightly overweight. A better style would be one with lots of hair, to counterbalance a larger body.

Short hair can be difficult to manage, as it can easily flop or go flat. Medium-length hair is the most flattering of all but needs to be well cut and kept in superb condition.

Long hair is the most versatile but is unflattering to many and only really looks good if it has weight and bulk.

Choose a style that complements your face shape. To compensate for a round face, find a style that gives height and fullness on top and proportionately less at the sides. A long face needs more width and less height with, perhaps, a little hair covering the forehead. If you have a square face, choose a style that allows some of the hair to break the line of the forehead, cheeks or jaw.

Like make-up, your hairstyle should em-phasize your good features and minimize the bad ones. Pull back your hair to reveal your best features, such as big eyes, or cover up areas where there is too little or too much of a good thing, such as a heavy brow. If you have a prominent nose, make it less noticeable by building up the crown and narrowing the line of the hair into the neck. If you have a receding chin, decide on a style that gives fullness at the nape of the neck and keeps the crown area relatively flat in order to balance the shape of the head.

THE CLASSIC BOB

The bob has proved the most popular and versatile of styles over the years. It goes from sporty to sophisticated with the greatest of ease.

Straight, fine hair is best for a blunt-cut, bob style, which will show off healthy hair. To keep it looking sleek and shiny, however, you'll need a trim every four to six weeks as well as regular conditioning treatments. Keep the length well above the shoulders or the simplicity of line is broken.

LONG AND WAVY

If you have thick, curly hair don't wear it too short, otherwise it can be unmanageable. But do have it carefully cut as this can make all the difference as to whether it looks fantastic or just frizzy.

It's best not to impose a particular style on thick, curly or wavy hair but rather to go with the natural swing of things. Layered cuts are also suitable for thick hair as they create shape and eliminate heaviness.

Straight or wavy, long hair is not the forget-about-it option it was once thought to be; if it's neglected. it soon looks dreary. It demands constant care, including a regular trim.

The 80's has seen the start of a more adventurous approach to hair treatments. The mood of the decade started with casual, carefree looks designed to fit into our busy lifestyles. Then the more outlandish styles and colours that started life at young street fashion level were gradually filtered down to a level acceptable for most of us.

In addition to a good cut, gels, mousses, setting lotions and hairsprays have all played a part in achieving the fullness and texture that is characteristic of the new looks. Gels and mousses, which can be applied on wet or dry hair, texturize hair and give it extra body. Both are good for reshaping permed hair and giving it extra moisture. Gels tend to give hair a slightly wet look; like mousse, it has a built-in conditioner which adds a sheen. Setting lotions are perfect for hair that is inclined to be soft and flyaway and therefore needs help in making the style last longer. A strong setting lotion, applied just to the roots while still wet, will help to give fullness yet leave a natural appearance.

The new-look hairstyles have also demanded setting with hairspray, which has come back into fashion and been given an update. Gone is the old-fashioned image of hair lacquer, heavy and sticky to the touch; the new sprays now set hair with a finer, drier mist. Hairsprays come into their own in wet or windy weather, especially if you have fine, flyaway hair. They are also good for giving hair extra volume, particularly if it is short. Simply bend over and spray a light film on the underside of your hair, then stand up and brush it back into place.

You can have a lot of fun with gel and create something really individual. Here Isabella Rossellini, top model and daughter of Ingrid Bergman, sports a spiky hairstyle achieved with the aid of gel. A small amount is combed through the hair to be distributed evenly. The gel could equally well be used to create a slicked-back style.

Setting gel or mousse helps to give natural curls more body. A light perm (left) gives the hair more fullness and weight at the back. But for extra volume and curl the hair has been finger-dried by 'scrunching' or squeezing with the aid of mousse.

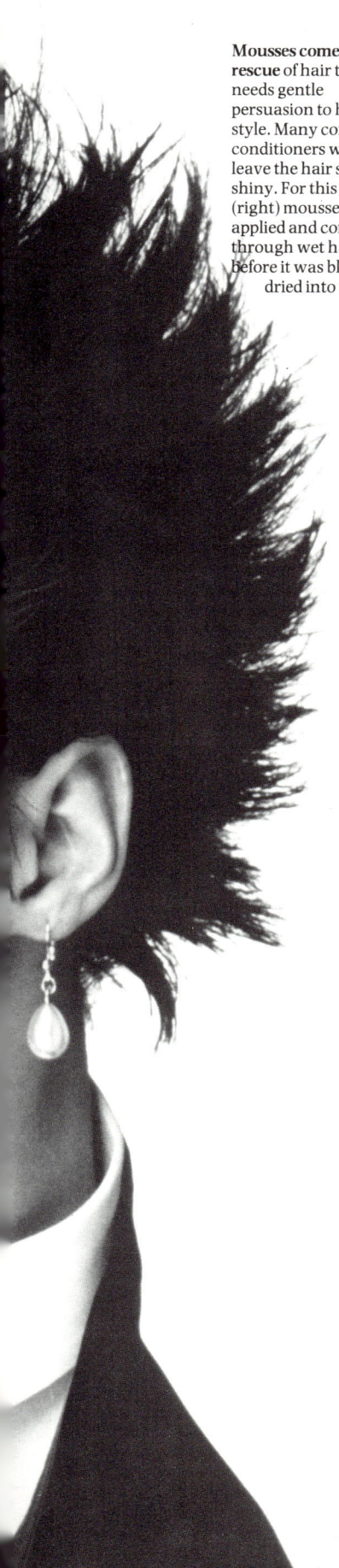

Mousses come to the rescue of hair that needs gentle persuasion to hold its style. Many contain conditioners which leave the hair soft and shiny. For this style (right) mousse was applied and combed through wet hair before it was blow-dried into shape.

TOOLS OF THE TRADE
Take advantage of the different electrical hairstyling tools around today. Designed to be used on hair that is already dry, they will give extra bounce or curl.

Curling tongs or styling wands will give the effect of anything from waves to tight ringlets. Many are now steam versions, which are gentler on the hair.

A hot styling brush is like a single hot roller on a handle. Use it to add body, create waves or curls and also to straighten short, layered hair.

Crimping irons work rather like a waffle iron. Clamp each section of hair in the crimper, then release it in turn.

Heated rollers are shaped like ordinary rollers but are used on dry hair to give curl, loose waves or bounce, depending on the size of the roller used.

The modern-day equivalent of grandma's rags are made of bendy rubber. Longer and more flexible than ordinary rollers, they can be wound round medium-length or long hair and left in for some time to create waves or curls.

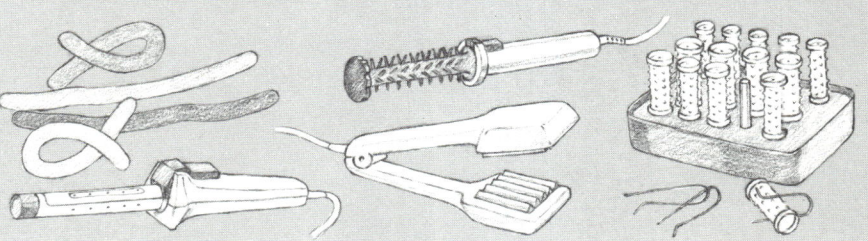

Whatever the length of your hair, it only takes a little imagination to change the style into a look that's right for day or night. Ask your hairdresser to show you different ways to wear your hair – or how to adapt the cut to give you greater scope.

Even a short style can be changed quite dramatically. You can wear it short and curly, short and spiky or short and smooth, with or without a fringe or simply sleeked back. Long hair can be put up, swept into huge waves and curls with tongs, or just worn loose. You can tie it back in a pony-tail, plait it or twist and roll it. Nothing makes a more elegant change for long hair than the classic chignon.

Whatever the limitations of your own hair, you can always add a hair extension. These are pieces of synthetic or real hair, either plaited, bound or left loose. Use them to give length and versatility to a short, growing-out style or to change a look that you are bored with.

Sometimes all you need to give a new look for evening is simply a new parting, a few pretty combs or pins, colourful slides, a ribbon or a bow, or even a feather or silk flower. To put a slide in your hair properly, push your hair forward into it for a fuller, more curvy look. To make a comb grip well, comb your hair through with it, sliding it in backwards, then turn it round and push it forward into the hair.

If you fancy a temporary change of colour, use one of the many spray-on hair colours or glitters that simply wash out.

The French pleat gives a sophisticated look for long hair. Using a soft bristle brush, smooth the back section of your hair over to one side of the head. Pin it in place with a straight row of grips, from the nape of the neck up to the bottom of the crown, to hold it smooth against the head. Leave the ends hanging loose. Pull up the back hair in the same way, then brush all the hair together, twisting it slightly. Roll it over into a pleat and secure with fine grips all the way up.

For the classic chignon, brush the hair back smoothly from the crown into a ponytail at the nape and secure. Twist round into a knot and fasten with fine hairpins round the outside. For a softer effect, pull a few side wisps of hair down and curl gently with tongs.

Pretty up long hair with headbands and scarves. One idea (bottom) for daytime is to brush the hair off the face and keep it in place with a headband, while the back of the hair is secured into a neat ponytail at the nape of the neck.

Adapt the look for evening with a pretty scarf (below), using hair gel combed through the hair for extra staying power. Tie the scarf around the crown of the head, fastening it into a bow at the front. Brush the loose hair at the nape of the neck up and over the scarf at the back; secure it in place.

STYLISH EXTRAS

Evening hairstyles can be either sophisticated or just plain fun. Here are a few ideas, using hair accessories of different kinds, to suit most styles of hair.

Use hair extensions to add just a few long strands to short hair, or one long strand at the side of a French pleat. A few dreadlocks can be fixed around the hairline to soften.

To combine the classic with the creative, take long hair off the face, secure it into a bun at the nape of the neck and dress it up with a snood. If you don't have enough hair to fill the snood, take an old hair-piece and secure it into your own hair to give the necessary bulk. If you don't have one, use cotton wool or a piece of soft material. First put your hair into a ponytail, and fix a circle of cotton wool round the top with grips. Then pull your hair round the outside of the cotton wool and over it; secure with grips into a loose bun. Or you can plait long hair, interweaving strands with a bright ribbon.

Short and long hair can be slicked back and a large bow or comb fixed near the nape of the neck.

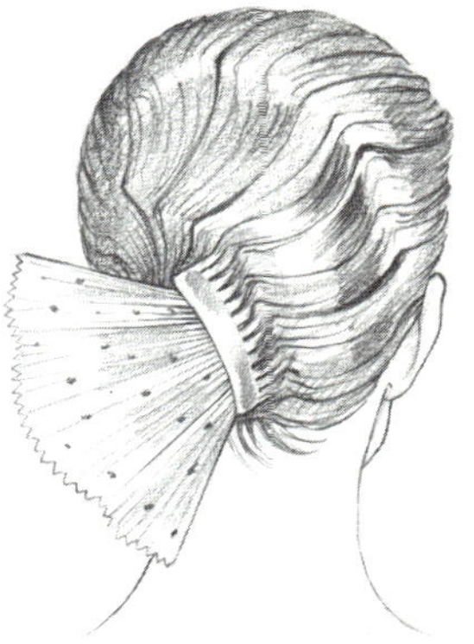

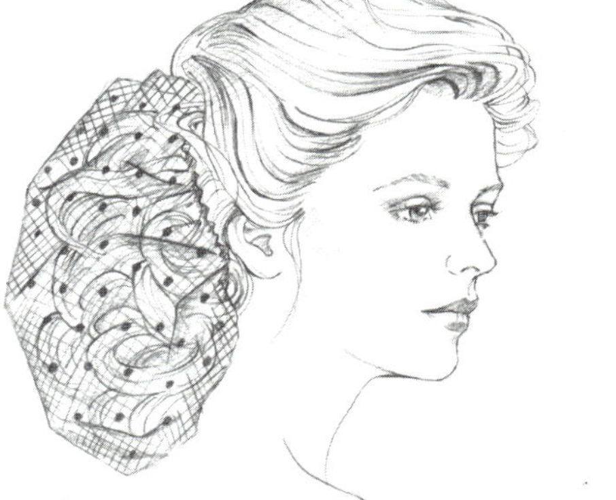

MAKING THE MOST OF YOUR SHAPE

Welcome back hats – all is forgiven. Forsaken for the last two decades, since bouffant hairstyles made them redundant in the 60's, hats are right back in favour in the eclectic 80's – not only with the 'patron saint of milliners', the Princess of Wales, and her followers, but with high stylists everywhere.

It's not just formal hats that have been given a new lease of life, but the everyday titfer too. Simple shapes in straw, felt, cotton and fake fur are lending importance and individuality to girls who have discovered that certain presence that only a hat can give them. While some hats are frivolous and decorative and some demand attention, others are practical weather-beaters. Why not invest in a felt bowler to pull on and protect your hair from showers? And as we lose 30 per cent of body heat from the top of our heads, pop on a beanie in frosty weather.

A well-chosen hat will complement, not overshadow, your personality so the shape you choose is fundamental. With no set rules, it's a case of trying on as many designs as possible to find the one that best suits your face, figure, hairstyle and frame of mind. Shape far outweighs decoration. Get the silhouette right and then think about the trim or lack of it.

Always view the result in a full-length mirror to gauge the total silhouette. Top milliner Patricia Underwood stresses that 'a hat should be part of a complete outfit, which should work from top to toe. The hat is there to balance the waistline, the neck-line, the hem.'

Pay attention to the proportions of a hat. The crown should fit accurately, so it's the brim or trim that should balance your body. If you are big and want a small hat, choose one with veiling or decoration to add width. If you are small, don't attempt too big a brim or you'll look swamped. As a general rule, unless you are very tall don't choose a brim that is wider than your shoulders. A wide hatband will break the crown, emphasize the brim and make your head look smaller.

Designer hats come with extravagant price tags. They are hand-made, with costly trimmings, and involve an enormous amount of work. With more dash than cash, you need wit and imagination as well as a disciplined hand to transform a simple straw into a stunner that will defy anyone to guess at its cost. Many of the inexpensive hats sold in large chain stores are ruined by cheap and gaudy trims. Remove them and you'll often find a classical elegant shape. The easiest way to achieve maximum chic with a limited budget is to use a top-designer trick and spray your basic straw

Ralph Lauren uses soft, natural straw for a floppy-brimmed, face-framing hat. It's a versatile shape: slick back the brim with a hat pin for a subtle souwester, unfurl it for a sun-shader or secure the brim front and back for a jaunty, pirate's crown.

The tricorne hat is a firm favourite with the Princess of Wales. It frames her face, works well with her hairstyle, flatters from every angle and doesn't add height.

❛ **The three-cornered hat is utterly charming on the Princess – it makes her look like the principal boy. No one had worn a tricorne for over twenty years, so as well as being a style that suits her immensely, it is also one that she could make her signature.** ❜

John Boyd

John Boyd
MILLINER TO THE PRINCESS OF WALES

with glossy or enamel paint.

For something a little fancier, you'll need to add your own decoration. Renovate a straw boater with dried flowers and grasses – the charming result can be a winner for the young. And judiciously placed bunches of silk flowers (in one colour or shades of the same – and not too many) atop a striking straw make the perfect face-framer for the grown-up woman.

● Don't wear a hat that is uncomfortable. You wouldn't squeeze a size 8 foot into a size 5 shoe, so don't necessarily expect a borrowed hat to fit you.

● A straw brim filters light and its colour is reflected on your face. Compensate with make-up (and avoid green brims).

● Rub dry bread or fine sandpaper over a felt hat to lift marks.

● If you want a man's-styled hat, buy one. Don't settle for a feminine imitation which will usually be of inferior quality.

The simplest hat shapes take well to sophistication. Sonia Rykiel gives a Basque beret a bow and a bauble and it yearns for a veil.

Face-framing halo

Practical panama

Stylish toque

A brim full of curls

Wrap up in a turban

Saucer hat

Modern usage of the words shirt and blouse denote that a shirt is tailored and a blouse is, well, blousy – but they are words that cover literally hundreds of variations. The simple classic shirt is a direct steal from the collar and cuffs design of male dressing – square in shape with narrow, cuffed sleeves and buttons running down the front from the neckline. Blouses are generally softer, fuller and more feminine in style.

The shirt or blouse is an integral part of any wardrobe and probably the one that gets the most wear, teaming as it does with trousers and skirts, sweaters and suits. It can be casual and sporty, crisp and businesslike or sexy and glamorous.

You can match the tempo of an outfit with a shirt or blouse or make an impact by contrast: a blouse with a pussy-cat bow at the neck will soften the effect of stark separates, a puritan collar looks fresh with denims and a simple chemise prevents a flounced peasant skirt looking over-fussy.

Simply-styled tops lend themselves to bright colours and fancy patterns. And as they tend to be the least costly element in an outfit they are the most practical ones to choose as high fashion items. An exotic print shirt adds verve and wit to investment basics without limiting their life.

There is a simple arithmetic to follow when you choose a top to suit your shape. Based on the all-important idea of balance, it is something that you can train your eye to recognize at a glance. Take sleeves, for instance: flabby upper arms can be disguised in loose shapes but narrow sleeves are best with a big bust. Everyone can wear long sleeves, but it is worth noting that a wide cuff shortens the look of the arm. A $\frac{3}{4}$-length sleeve is unflattering on long arms and a short sleeve widens the silhouette.

Consider necklines carefully. A soft cowl, a V or a stand-away line will lengthen the neck, while high or oriental collars will exaggerate a heavy chin. Wide collars will give the impression of a smaller waistline and a sailor collar will emphasize a big bust.

The indispensable white shirt can be adapted to suit all shapes. This soft style is tailor-made for the hippy or angular figure and has a slimming effect on the well-rounded.

□ ○ ⊗ △

Feel fragile and pretty in a delicate blouse. This smock shape, falling in soft folds of fabric from a wide boat neckline and horizontally designed collar, adds and enhances curves. If you prefer to minimize your shapeliness and still look romantic, choose a blouse with seams that slim the midriff and remove excess fullness.

Clean and collarless

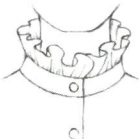

Romantic and ruffled

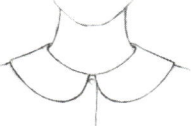

Peter Pan style

The width of a rever, the length of a collar or the fullness of a sleeve are the details that spell fashion's current handwriting; they are also the details that date. Even a seemingly classic shirt can look sadly out of style if the points of its collar or design of its sleeve go out of favour.

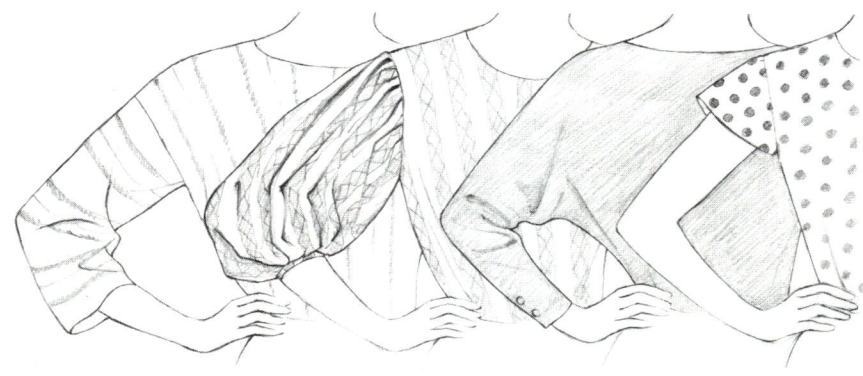

Unstructured   **Pretty and puffed**   **Deep dolman**   **Extending cap**

You can make a top from scraps of tinfoil, rags and bones, a pack of cards, rolls of ribbon or even a plastic bag – and over the years some of our most innovative and respected designers have done just that. Alternative dressing is the fun side of fashion; who is to say that you can't bind up your body in bandages or wrap up in rubber if that's the look you choose to wear and the one that makes you happy?

When a new and often eccentric look hits the high-fashion headlines or erupts on to the streets, the conservative shake their heads in despair. But amazingly quickly the new proportions and cuts are watered down to a palatable level and even the most disbelieving find themselves longing for a wrap-around inspired by the Orient, a space-age tabard or a T-shirt that owes much of its appeal to a bin liner. From there it's a short step to quite happily hacking out the neck of a treasured sweatshirt or putting your bed linen on your back by transforming it into a ragknit.

Funky fashions lend themselves best to tops. It's easier to experiment with tube knits, T-shirts and square cuts than skirts and trousers where irregularities of cut and design seem much more daring. As far as shapes go, the trick is always to keep the body beautiful in mind – a flash of flesh or gently contoured curves will curb all suggestion that freakiness is unsexy.

A fashionably fresh design can also cover a multitude of sins. Keyhole cuts invent new and often flattering erogenous zones for women who may not choose to bare or reveal the more acceptably sensual areas, and tubular shapes are kind to hefty hips, wide waists and bountiful busts alike. And while a sparky, spanking new design doesn't have to dominate your dress, it can be bold and bizarre enough to make your body size not only immaterial, but open only to guesswork.

□ ○ ▽ △

Rip faded frocks or remnants of favourite fabric into rags and you'll give them a new lease of life. To make a recycled ragknit, simply rip your fabric into strips 1in (2.5cm) wide. Knot them together, then roll into a ball. Using stocking stitch, knit the 'yarn' into squares then stitch them together in the shape of a casual T-shaped top.

It couldn't be easier and it's nice to know that every piece of fabric has its own story to tell.

□ ○ ▽ △

When it comes to clothes inspired by Japanese workwear, doubling up on shirts can be twice as nice. Keep the colours clear and simple, and let the shapes and prints hog the limelight. See how ethnic, square-cut shapes can be cool and covered-up or minimally bared.

Knitwear conjures up visions of warm and sensible winter woollies for the top half of the body. But nowadays the perennial wool classics are living happily side by side with a whole new generation of pullovers, cardigans, slipovers and knitted tops that come in every fashion guise and in dozens of different yarns. At the top there is cashmere, the 'Queen Bee' of knitting wools, down to the more humble, man-made 'workers' that are excellent at keeping their shape even though the feel isn't quite so royal. And in the middle is cotton – a yarn that knits up into deliciously scrunchy sweaters that improve with age.

Knitwear is supple and soft and envelops the body; it has a softening effect on the small, but a tendency to make the large look larger. If you are well-rounded, or big all over, wear your sweaters on the large side and disguise flabby upper arms with batwing or kimono-style sleeves.

Evening sweaters in angora, cashmere or mohair – beaded, embroidered, pailleted or appliquéed – are perfect when you want to sparkle but not look overdressed.

● Put an angora sweater in the fridge for 24 hours to stop the fluff coming off.

● The simplest way to transform a classic sweater is with shoulder pads. Sew Velcro on to the pads and they'll sit secure, giving a fashionable silhouette.

● A big bulky sweater doubles as a jacket, but if you are small don't choose too big a design as chunky textures and bold patterns will swamp a petite figure.

A sleeveless slipover is a great asset, given the layered nature of today's dressing. This short, cotton Fairisle version is a smart fashion for anyone who is small on top – it will round them out.

Designer hand-knit sweaters are the latest fashion status symbol. There's a lot of work involved in them and a sweater like this with its intricate cable panels, stripes and zigzags comes with an accordingly high price tag. But if you can bribe your granny or take to the needles yourself, you'll have the classiest looks at a fraction of the price.

KNITTED NECKLINES

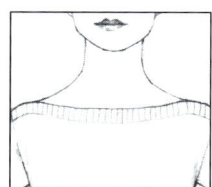

A slash neck focuses the silhouette on the shoulders.

A V neck flatters a big bust, a round face and a short neck.

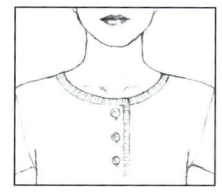

A grandad's vest with its shallow neckline elongates the neck.

Soften a harsh crew or jewel neck with a shirt, scarf or chain.

A deep cowl demands a long neck.

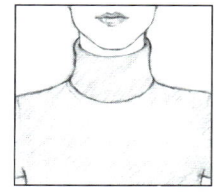

A polo or round neckline minimizes a wide neck.

□ ○ ▽ △

**Forget the functional,
knitted-jacket image of
the cardigan** and think
about sensual layers.
This peach lambswool
cardigan with its
plunging V and low-
buttoning welt has
superbly simple, fluid
lines. Worn with the
right separates, it
should appeal to most
proportions, but here it
is seen at its model girl
best.

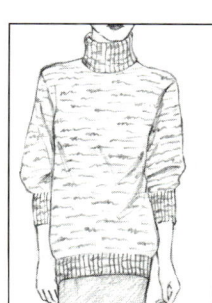

The long, lean sweater
– hip-length or longer –
stretches out a round
figure and overlooks a
big bust.

**The short, cropped
sweater** is great news
for a good waist, but
bad news for a good
bust.

51

With any controversy about hem lengths long since dead, we wear the skirts we like and the ones that suit us. Skirts show off the legs and put the focus on how good their proportions are. If you are longer than average from knee to ankle you've got nothing to worry about, but a little camouflage may help the less fortunate. On the knee – where the thigh tapers in, but before the knee bulges out – is traditionally the most flattering length. Unless your legs are superb, avoid very pale or eye-catching legwear with shorter skirts.

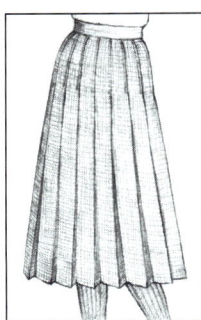

Stitched-down pleats hug the body, but be sure they don't release at your widest point.

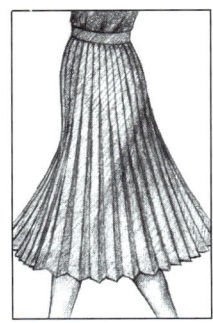

Knife-sharp and permanent, sunray pleating gives a skirt great movement and swing.

Soft, unpressed pleats falling from a stitched-in waistband give the fullness of a dirndl without the flounce.

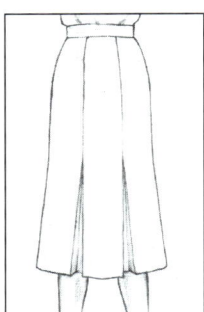

With the long, lean line, box pleats give ease of movement without distracting from the tubular effect.

The width and fullness of a dirndl skirt will make stocky legs look slimmer by comparison. But to wear a *very* big skirt you need height and not too many curves. Avoid full skirts if you are busty or rounded.

IN PROPORTION

It's the shape of the skirt rather than its length that dictates the fashion line. The bottom-huggers, that come up ribbed and skinny, need the longer length to balance their lean lines, whereas the ra ra, for instance, made its impact as a combination of frills and a jaunty half-mast crop. Proportion is, as ever, the vital element. Designers continuously alter the proportions in subtle ways, so it is important to watch that your lengths and breadths don't date you.

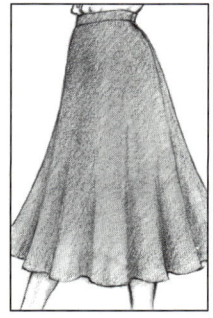 

A full-circle skirt takes a lot of fabric. Let it swish in something soft and light, not bulky and bulk-making.

A dropped Basque gives a flat, trim line across the tummy. But it's not a good choice for the bottom-heavy.

 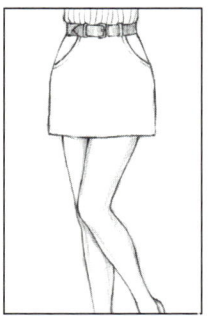

A flared or flounced short skirt made in sweatshirting is a sporty option, at home by the beach or pool.

A mini skirt is shortest and sweetest. But it's an abbreviated crop that doesn't suit those of mature years.

Short and sharp is the skinny silhouette of the knee-grazing skirt. Not only is it slimming to every figure shape, but it's smart, slick and sexy too – especially with a revealing slit.

Freedom, equality and domination – metaphorically speaking, wearing the trousers, means a whole lot more than just striding out in something sensible or comfortable. But with the battles over what we should, or must, wear fought long ago, wearing trousers is now every woman's right. But whether every woman is right to do so is quite a different matter.

If you are well-proportioned, you can easily adapt to any extreme, from jodhpurs to patio pants or from Oxford bags to stretch ski-pants. But if you feel your figure needs a little help, pick your trousers with care.

To find a trouser shape to suit your figure its's a case of experimenting with as many different shapes as you can find. Try several sizes on too – trousers that are too tight accentuate both the under- and the overweight. Bear in mind that turn-ups, or cuffs, will shorten the appearance of the leg and a high waist increases its apparent length.

Don't be fooled by tight jeans. They may appear (by acting like a corset) to slim you down in the fitting room, but after a couple of hours' wear, your body heat will produce horizontal stress lines that emphasize any problem spots like hips or thighs. A little loose – not baggy – is best.

Always use a rear view mirror when trying on. You may choose to ignore a backside that's not up to par, but if you flaunt it in ill-fitting trousers, no one else will have a chance to. If you are bottom-heavy, avoid trousers in bulky fabrics such as heavy tweed or raised-pile velour. Go for slimming, flat fabrics like flannel, gabardine, jersey and silk.

Trousers are one instance where 'borrowing from the boys' is not a good idea. Quite apart from the differing waist and hip sizes, women are generally longer from waist to crotch than men, so it's rare to find a man's tailored trouser that will give an accurate fit.

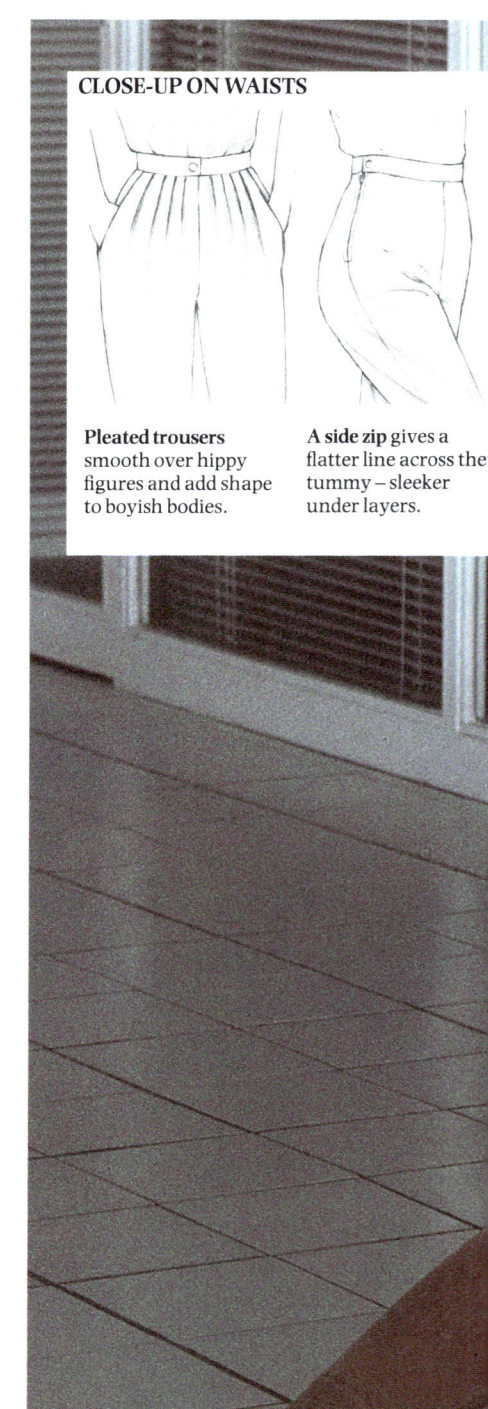

CLOSE-UP ON WAISTS

Pleated trousers smooth over hippy figures and add shape to boyish bodies.

A side zip gives a flatter line across the tummy – sleeker under layers.

The narrow proportion is an all-round flatterer and these slimline ski-pants (right) give a lean look which can be dressed up or down. Add a high heel for glamour or switch to a baseball boot for action days.

The classic, straight-legged style of trouser (left), with side pockets and two soft front pleats, probably suits more people than any one other style. The cut and fit of a pair of trousers is crucial so it's worth investing in the most expensive pair of classic ones your budget will allow.

A high waist
lengthens the legline
but emphasizes a
short waist or large
bust.

A drawstring or
elasticated waist is
great for wide or
fluctuating
waistlines.

Boys may long to get out of short trousers, but girls are panting to get into them. Abbreviated trousers and short or long shorts have become firm fashion favourites.

Trousers that fall short come in every conceivable shape from sawn-offs through breeches, zouaves, shorts, culottes, gauchos and bloomers and there is a style to suit all of our shapes. But before you chop up your classic trousers stop and think because, more than any other items, these are the ones that need extra careful proportioning.

Initially most hippy or bigger girls are wary of them, but they really aren't just for string-bean figures, they're flattering for broad beans too. But to combine cropped pants with ample curves you have to balance the silhouette. Printed trousers in subdued, dark shades will diminish if you team them with a light plain top. Textures balance the figure too – so wear a chunky, knitted top with sleek cotton over the curves. Emphasize a slim waist and well-turned ankles – who then would notice your backside?

Cropped trousers cut the legs more than any other style, which is great for the leggy, but means more work for the short-limbed. The easiest cheat is to cut back on colour mixing to take the definition out of the breaks. And if you're very short, go for the sleekest, slimmest fitting trousers your figure can take.

Abbreviated trousers are a bonus if you are very busty. As long as you wear shirts that pare down your top half, nature has already done the balancing act. But beware over-voluminous shapes which merely make you look big all over. Very skinny styles tend to make the busty look top-heavy, of course, so aim for interest at the neckline or a bust-ignoring tunic to look sensational in pedal pushers.

The short crops are complemented by flat shoes, but for smarter occasions a mid-heel court or pump, especially if it tones with trousers and stockings, gives elegance to this basically tomboy look.

Short trousers team best with very short or very long jackets. Anything in between, like a classic blazer, looks out of tune – a half-hearted attempt at a different silhouette. Short shapes give a boxy line, and the leanness of the extended jacket not only pares off the pounds but also hides trouser seats that don't fit perfectly.

□ ○ ▽ △

The loose colonial style of shorts is easy for everyone. Take care with its partnerships: the bloused top is good for skinny and hippy girls alike but should be tucked in or worn unbelted by the rounded or top-heavy.

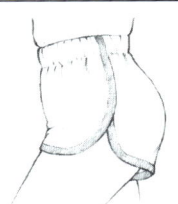

High-cut running shorts lengthen the legline – but only flaunt this much flesh if it is fit and firm.

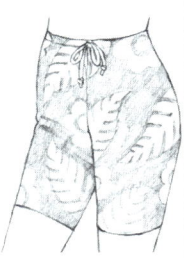

Sleek bermudas give a sporty, leggy look. Not the most flattering shape – make sure your legs can take it.

Tailored shorts are the safe crop. Chic and coordinated, they look trim and slick in the city.

Lopped-off legs look as good on round bottoms as they do on the more fashionably androgynous. Baggy cropped trousers worn anywhere from just below the knee to a fraction above the ankle are the hippy girl's surprise friend, especially if accompanied by a cut-off top. They are also a success for the well-proportioned round figure and perfect for the skinny – though too voluminous for the top-heavy. This is a perfect illustration of tricks with line: what adds bulk to some figure shapes strips it from others.

Bloomers give a soft line but are not for the rounded, whose curves need no emphasis.

Pedal pushers are skintight and sexy. They look stunning on those without an inch of spare flesh, lumpy on the rest.

Knickerbockers do wonders for heavy thighs, especially if the ankles are worthy of a turn.

57

MAKING THE MOST OF YOUR SHAPE

Today if anything dates a woman more than her clothes, it's her hose. The greatest give-away is a boring pair of flesh-coloured or tan legs.

Contemporary fashions demand a wardrobe of styles – opaques and textures for workdays, colourful sheers for smarter occasions, witty patterns, motifs and graffiti messages for fun days, and dazzling metallics and shiny paillettes on sexy black sheers for starry nights.

And the good news is that most of us can wear most styles. Obviously a horizontal-hoop stripe needs careful consideration, and only a few should attempt pale, thick-textured tights, but the new classics – opaques and gossamer sheers in every shade imaginable – suit all of us. And textured tights (which also come in support styles) can act as a camouflage for varicose veins, scars or blemishes, as well as a fashion accessory.

Your legs can change the mood of an outfit. Experiment with the effects: knubbly tights, for instance, will give a cord skirt a casual feel, lacy tights a more upbeat mood. Complement your clothes with coloured legs. Unless the colour of your tights matches that of your shoes, go for darker shoes to tights.

STOCKINGS OR TIGHTS?

Tights were not an invention of the mini-skirt generation. Apart from ballet dancers' tights, which provided a prototype, the thick, wool variety already existed for sportswear. The brevity of the mini skirt simply instigated the transformation of tights into fine deniers.

Tights quickly superseded stockings, which was hardly surprising considering their advantages. They are far sleeker under clothes and they eliminate any gaps, as well as being immeasurably more comfortable and, especially in their heavier weights, far warmer in winter. Stockings are, however, more hygienic to wear, as they allow air to circulate more freely. Tights do also work out more expensive – if you snag one leg the pair is ruined, whereas with stockings you can always match up pairs.

But romance, not finance, is stockings' allure. Ask most men how they feel about suspenders or watch the way their eyes follow a neat pair of stockinged legs and it is patently clear why stockings haven't disappeared altogether. Along with nostalgic undies, stockings are quite simply sexier – and for a special dinner or date, isn't that worth just a little discomfort?

- Wash your tights after every wear. It will not only get them clean, but also restore their elasticity.

- Bulk-buy tights in your basic shades so that you're never unexpectedly caught out.

- You can halt a run with clear nail varnish or soap, but if it's important to look good, it's important to carry a spare pair of tights.

- Dispense with, or separate out (for wearing under trousers), any damaged tights. A drawer full of faulty nylons will not remind you to re-stock.

- Denier is the hosiery term for density – the lower the figure the finer the hose.

- Choose tights with a sheer sandal heel and toe to wear with strappy sandals or slingback shoes.

- Pop socks, fine denier for under trousers and long skirts, are especially useful for maternity.

- Wear control-top tights containing lycra to make you sleek under sweater dresses and the sheerest of fabrics.

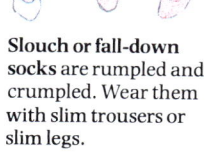

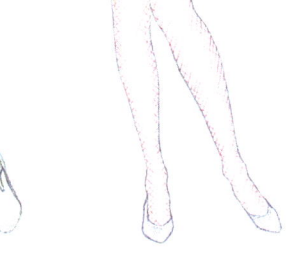

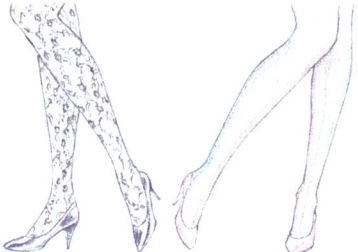

Horizontal-hoop tights emphasize stunning, skinny legs and short, stumpy ones.

Slouch or fall-down socks are rumpled and crumpled. Wear them with slim trousers or slim legs.

The fully-fashioned seamed stocking is only sexy as long as the seams are straight.

Fishnets have cast off their tarty image. Buy them in all the brightest, vibrant hues.

Lacy tights, the fashion phenomenon of the early 80's, are still pretty for evenings.

Bi-coloured or split-personality legs add wit to slim calves.

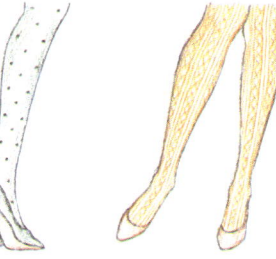

Animal prints are fun and young – but they lose their charm if your legs aren't.

Decorated stockings with bows or paillettes divert the eye to a shapely ankle.

Bright, bold coloured legs are the slickest route to a pulled-together outfit.

Dotty tights are best in black. In paler shades they can look like a disease.

Textured tights put warm legs into vogue and carry a wintry feel through from top to toe.

Legwarmers balance up a big body and fill in a gap if your trousers don't quite meet up.

The ultimate in bold legwear is Norma Kamali's 'washing instruction' tights. Designed for her OMO collection, they are silly and great fun. Don't let your clothes compete for attention – they couldn't possibly win. Instead wear them (as shown) with simple separates and let your legs steal the show.

Looking at most modern shoes you could be forgiven for thinking that they were designed by someone who had heard of a human foot, but never seen one. What else could explain why shoes are made with such little regard for the bone structure they encase and, more pertinently, why they appear to be designed for a foot that has its longest toe in the middle?

Basic design faults apart, shoes and boots are one of fashion's strongest tools. The total mood, proportion and balance of an outfit depends on the right choice of shoes – and if you treat shoes simply as an afterthought it always shows. When it comes to attuning our eyes to a new style, what you wear on your feet can be the most significant element – particularly in adjusting to new proportions. The wrong pair of shoes can ruin the whole impact of a new outfit.

The choice of footwear available is huge, but what we actually wear has more to do with current trends than with what does or doesn't flatter. With a few exceptions – like no spindly straps and skyscraper heels on very large women, nor ankle straps on those with wide ankles – there are no rules. Shoes should obviously be chosen for comfort but also to suit our lifestyle and clothes rather than our figure shapes.

HOVERING HEEL HEIGHTS

Looking back over the years it seems remarkable that fashion-conscious women appear to have had so little say in the height of heel they wore.

When designers dictated height we all learnt to run for buses in teetering heels or crippling platform soles. And when the fashions demanded flatties, our feet and our doctors sighed with relief. Before our eyes became properly accustomed to flat shoes we may have felt dumpy and plump in them but comfort and sanity soon ruled and we quickly forgot how to walk downstairs in heels – and in any case found them vulgar. When the direction changes again we will, no doubt, step back onto our stilts and relegate the flat soles to sportswear.

The trainer phenomenon is another matter altogether. Once we all discovered how great they felt with jogging suits or jeans we invented ways to wear them with our other clothes. If you are going to walk some distance or if you are going to be on your feet all day it makes sense to wear something comfortable. Copy chic New York Yuppies (Young Urban Professionals) who walk to work in their jogging shoes and change into smart pumps once they've reached their destination.

- The key to a classic shoe is lack of exaggeration or unnecessary detail.

- Bright coloured shoes are just as useful as dark wintry shades – and are seasonless.

- Bold shoe shades need to be repeated in your clothes, preferably near the face. So if you want to wear red shoes, add a red scarf or necklace.

- Low-cut or pale-coloured shoes make feet look longer.

- If you're small, avoid very high heels or you'll look as though you're on stilts. And if you're very tall don't think you always have to wear flatties.

- Shoes with ankle straps shorten the leg by visually cutting off the foot.

- Always try on both shoes of a pair; it's quite common for one foot to be slightly larger than the other.

- Don't buy shoes when you are hot as your feet will be slightly swollen.

- To ensure comfort, always fit a shoe to the broadest part of your foot.

   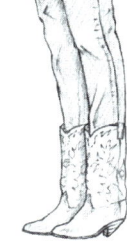  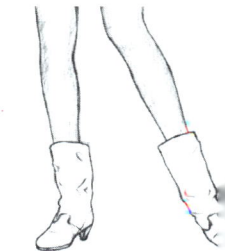

The flat-heeled, knee-high riding boot is a fashion collectible that never dates.

Flat, lace-up skating-style boots are light enough to wear with lean skirts as well as trousers.

Knee-high, high-heeled boots swing in and out of favour, so they look either very smart or very dated.

The cowboy boot is never out of style, but sometimes out of place. Keep it clean and casual.

Bouncy bumper boots – laced-up and rubber soled – are sporty and supremely comfortable.

Canvas boots, lightweight and cool, can be any shape. Here they are mid-heeled and mid-calf.

 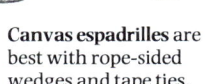  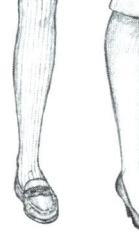 

Wear ballet slippers in kid or canvas for day, switch to satin or velvet by night.

Wedge sandals give you height but keep your feet flat and happy.

Canvas espadrilles are best with rope-sided wedges and tape ties.

The casual leather loafer is structured on a stiff sole, but more supple on a rubber one.

The classic court shoe: almond-toed and mid-heeled. Buy the best quality you can afford.

A strappy summer sandal can double up as an evening shoe.

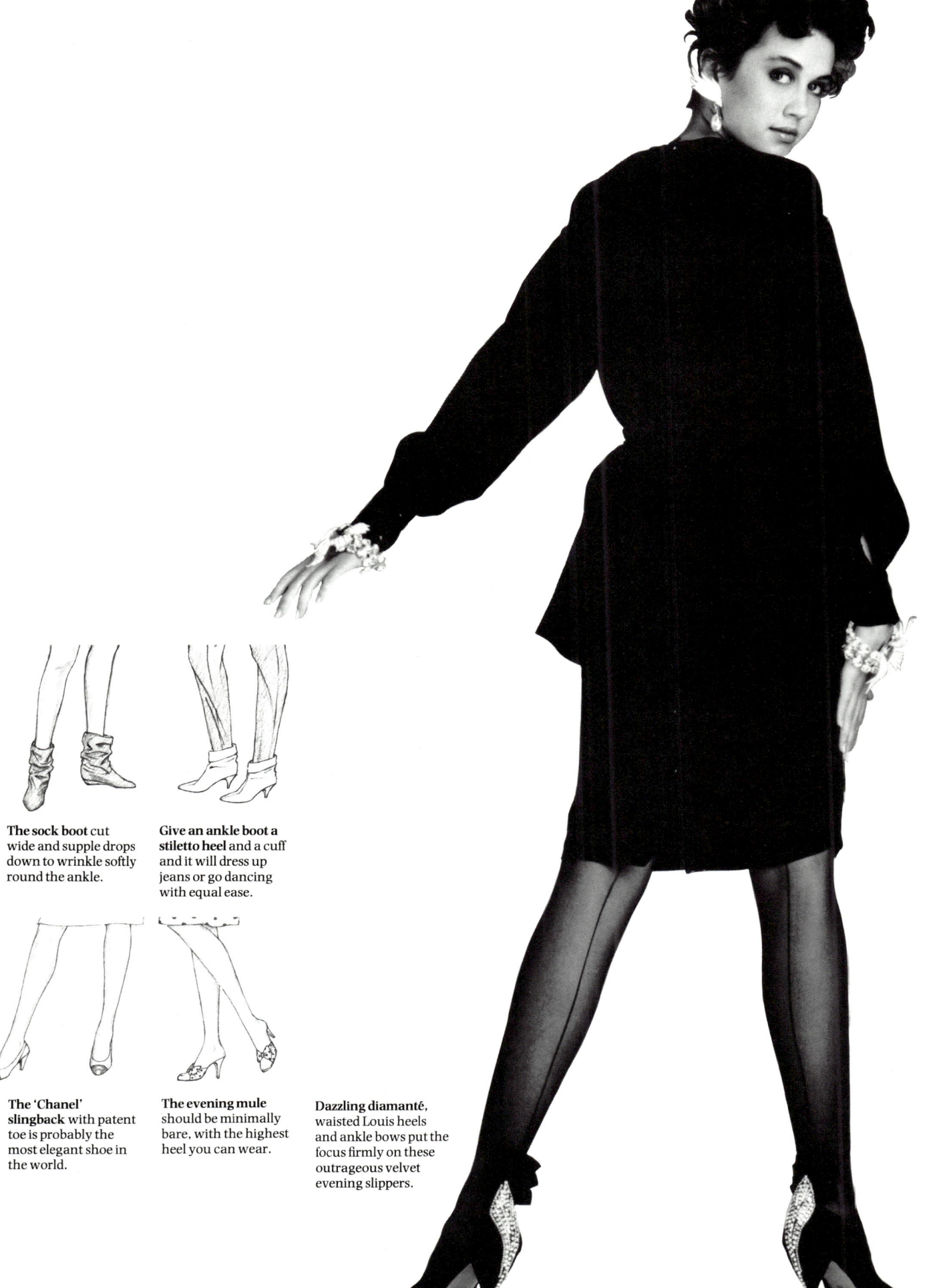

The sock boot cut wide and supple drops down to wrinkle softly round the ankle.

Give an ankle boot a stiletto heel and a cuff and it will dress up jeans or go dancing with equal ease.

The 'Chanel' slingback with patent toe is probably the most elegant shoe in the world.

The evening mule should be minimally bare, with the highest heel you can wear.

Dazzling diamanté, waisted Louis heels and ankle bows put the focus firmly on these outrageous velvet evening slippers.

61

A winter coat is probably the largest single investment in any wardrobe. It is also the one garment likely to get the most wear, so it makes sense to allow a generous proportion of your annual clothes budget for its purchase. It must be something you will be happy to wear almost every day of the winter, sometimes several winters: a good coat can be expected to be part of your wardrobe for much longer than most day clothes.

With this in mind it makes sense to opt for a classic shape with the minimum of fashionable but datable detailing. There are basically four classic shapes: the tailored, double-breasted coat, which falls slim and straight to the knee; the trenchcoat, originally designed as weather protection for soldiers in the trenches, with its square shoulders and functional epaulettes and storm flaps; the single-breasted, man's-style overcoat with raglan sleeves; and the simple wrap-over with its own tie belt.

When considering which shape of coat is best for you, it is essential to have an eye for the proportions. Wide shoulders lend importance to almost every shape and flatter most figures as they have the effect of minimizing the waistline. Take care, though – if the shoulders are over-accentuated, they can appear too mannish on a trenchcoat and rather overpowering on a simple wrap.

Length, too, depends on the shape of the coat. A belted style needs the extra length and vice versa in untailored coats – a loose-fitting coat worn unbelted can give the wearer a waif-like appearance. A shorter-length coat is always better in a body-skimming shape.

As far as body shapes go, if you are tall and slim you can wear most styles, but a belted or slightly waisted design is least likely to create a beanpole effect. If you are very short, avoid belted styles and opt instead for the simplest, least fussy shape you can find. While fussiness drowns a small person, it also sits awkwardly on a woman of fuller proportions. It is generally a good idea to avoid extraneous detail on a coat: any over-emphasis, whether it is on the lapels, collar or cuffs, rarely flatters and it always dates.

All coats profit from being worn on the large side. Try on a size or two larger than you might expect and you will discover that the coat will usually sit and fall better. A generous cut prevents a tailored coat from looking over-formal or too strict. A looser fit can also prevent a cheap cloth looking skimpy or shabby and anything roomy always gives the impression of a slimmer body underneath. You can then add layers in cold weather without causing strain lines on the coat.

□ ○ ▽ ⊗

The tailored, double-breasted coat is the smartest, most formal classic shape. Its lines are slimming so it is a good choice if you are big. Slightly inset shoulders are flattering to the broad-shouldered.

Once you decide on a strictly tailored style, be prepared to spend a little extra. With tailored clothes, the quality and fit are more obvious and any imperfections are emphasized.

□ ○ ▽ △

A man's-style overcoat has loose, easy lines and a neat collar. Best worn on the large side, it suits those of average or above-average build but would drown girls who are short or have slight proportions.

The raglan sleeve, comfortable to wear, is not a good choice if you have very broad shoulders.

Soften the coat's mannish cut with feminine accessories such as this soft pink woollen scarf and leather gloves. Team it with good-quality, classic separates to strike a note of stylish but casual dressing.

If you choose this style, look for bargains among men's overcoats in second-hand clothes shops.

□ ○ ▽ △

In the traditional Burberry raincoat the styling details are an integral and essential part of the coat: the epaulettes, storm flaps and straps round the sleeves are functional for the rain and decorative whatever the weather.

When not being worn as serious rainwear, this classic coat benefits from being treated in a stylish but more casual way.

It can easily be worn by most figure shapes; leave it unbelted if you are short.

□ ✗ ▽ △

An ankle-grazing silk dressing gown, like this one by Lanvin, makes a more elegant evening topper than a wool coat.

The softly draped lines of the wrap-over make it the most feminine of the classic shapes. It is neat and uncluttered and flatters small women, while the belted style accentuates the narrow waist of tall, slim girls.

Aim to find a coat that will meet every demand of your life, without being over-smart or too casual for certain occasions. Your choice of coat is an important statement about yourself – it is usually the first thing you are seen in and the item that makes a lasting impression about your particular style, fashion sense and attitude. Don't be tempted to opt for a sleek, groomed style if you are not the type to carry this image through. Conversely, if you always dress elegantly, you will be ill at ease in something very casual.

Wool of one form or another is the obvious choice of fabric for a winter coat, from cashmere at the top, most luxurious end of the scale, through to tweed and gabardine. While there is something definitely superior about natural materials, the addition of a small percentage of man-made fibre can increase the life of the cloth and help maintain the coat's shape.

Choice of colour is of course subjective. A neutral such as navy, grey, camel or black is often the wisest option if you want a shade that tallies with the bulk of your wardrobe. A coat in a cheerful colour can make a surprise

impact, but a more practical way to introduce colour is the clever use of bright accessories.

A vividly coloured muffler or extravagantly patterned shawl can bring life to a sombre coat. Belts too can add a dash of difference: simply swop the coat's own self-fabric belt for a colourful or unusual leather belt. Gloves, bags and brightly coloured stockings and shoes will all come to the rescue of a subtle and subdued coat on days when you need a little light-heartedness in your life.

THE ALTERNATIVES

A coat is a topper and ideally should be long enough to cover any of your chosen hem lengths and sufficiently roomy to accommodate any extremes of design you happen to have in your wardrobe. However, if you wear a variety of shapes, as most of us do, it would be absurd to expect one coat to work with everything you own. You will also have to rely on shawls, jackets and inexpensive alternative coats to wear with your more unusual or individual clothes.

Of course it is not essential to buy a classic coat at all – some women would not dream of doing so. The season's particular fashion coats can be chic and stylish. They make a very welcome bonus to a wardrobe that already boasts a classic, go-anywhere coat, though by their very nature their life is limited. Fashionable coats often take their inspiration from ethnic origins – witness the swirling ponchos and ruana-style shawls – or are derivatives of sportswear, such as the padded duvet coat which has its roots in winter sport.

Improvisations come in here, as alternatives to the conventional coat. Government surplus stores offer a wide selection of unusual cover-ups at budget prices, from military greatcoats and naval jackets to nurses' capes. Try men's and boy's outfitters for other possibilities, such as an oversized man's dinner jacket, a tweed hacking jacket, or a plaid-wool dressing gown – shake off the bedroom image by changing the cord for a sturdy leather belt.

□ ○ ▽ △

The ruana, a Mexican-style shawl which is simplicity itself to wear, makes a fittingly casual cover-up over jeans. It looks equally good over a tailored suit or evening separates. Well-chosen accessories carry through the ethnic flavour of the shawl and stop the outfit looking drab.

DRESSING FOR YOUR LIFESTYLE

Only ever buy clothes based on YOUR needs, YOUR budget and YOUR priorities. And when it comes to dressing for occasions always under- rather than over-dress.

DRESSING FOR YOUR LIFESTYLE

The basics in your wardrobe are the clothes that you wear and wear. It is impossible to make a realistic list of the minimum requirements for a basic wardrobe because they differ for everyone, depending on their job, whether they live in town or country and their leisure activities – their whole way of life. What a schoolteacher regards as her basic clothes will differ from those of a receptionist in a smart hotel, just as the essential wardrobe of a lawyer or business executive will have little in common with that of a mother at home with three small children.

Basic means that you, and only you, can wear those clothes in a variety of ways. Even among people of similar lifestyles, important factors such as shape, colouring and personality have a great influence on their choice of basic clothes. This is what creates a personal style. A girl who likes the formality and suits the strictness of grey flannel may see no need to own a cowboy belt, an item that can be pivotal to the owner of casual jeans, ethnic skirts and dungarees.

If you work at or from home, you don't need a huge and varied wardrobe. But beware – when there are no appearances to keep up, it is all too easy to neglect yourself. It is still important to dress with self-respect and wear cheerful, refreshing clothes even if the only company you can expect all day is the plumber or the baby. If you dress like a slob, the chances are that whatever you are working at – be it housework, childcare or the great novel – you will approach in an equally slipshod manner.

You may well prefer the ease of trousers to skirts, but living in jeans gives you no variety, so choose some cords and well-cut flannels as well. On the same principle, get some good leather loafers to alternate with your sneakers.

> At times I dream of being impeccable. I say to myself, I'll go for suits and Hermès bags, but I never have the time or the will. I like the comfort of an old cashmere sweater, faded jeans, T-shirts softened by lots of wear and my Repetto ballet shoes. To be dressed in five seconds without thinking about it – that's my idea of luxury.

Jane Birkin
ACTRESS

PLAYCLOTHES

Mark the difference between work and play. Don't regard it as an extravagance to invest in some special weekend clothes – and make sure they are ones that simply won't work in your business environment. Beware of turning your old work clothes into your weekend outfit, those you no longer consider spruce or stylish enough for your work colleagues to see. They may be fine for gardening or washing the car, but the danger is that they can end up being worn socially all weekend. You spend your leisure time with the people who matter most to you – you husband, boyfriend, family or friends – so grace it with fresh, exciting clothes that make you feel great.

If your Monday to Friday uniform is discreet business suiting, choose some beautiful sweats, witty overalls or a great jogging suit. But if you wear jeans all week, go for something tailored or feminine instead.

At their most basic clothes are purely utilitarian, designed for warmth, comfort and modesty. It would be hard to find a much more practical garment than the jumpsuit – otherwise known as the siren suit, flying suit, boiler suit, all-in-one or overalls.

Here this many-titled suit is given fashionable handwriting by Jeff Banks. It spells leisure and relaxation, though its colour ensures that it's not *too* practical.

You don't have to look tough and scruffy in jeans. In a pair of worn denims with a man's shirt (fastened with silver cufflinks), a huge grey cardigan and a long scarf worn as a tie, Jane Birkin (left) looks as sexy as she looks relaxed and comfortable.

Getting dressed should always be a pleasure, not a headache: this applies just as much to the daily routine of dressing for work as to getting ready for a party. If you have a well-planned, colour-coordinated wardrobe, you're halfway there.

You'll find that interchangeable separates are the backbone of any business wardrobe, especially one that has to travel. As Gill Hewitt, director of Austin Reed's hugely successful women's venture Options confirms, 'All you really need is a skirt suit with coordinating trousers, two or three cotton shirts, several classic sweaters plus a few extras like silk or satin shirts for dressier business functions and a waistcoat to add layers. Buy one easy dress for the days when the arithmetic involved in separates dressing seems too complicated.' A general rule with separates is that the more of a matching outfit you put together, the more formal you'll appear.

To collect a basic office wardrobe that works, keep to a colour theme – navy, grey, black and beige being the accepted classics. Sharpen up your classic tones with white and give them wit with splashes of bright accent colour. A luxurious, cashmere muffler in baby pink or a wide glossy emerald belt will soon dispel the middle-of-the-road feel that basics can assume.

Nautical-inspired fashion trends crop up every three or four seasons, but a navy blazer never goes out of style. It's too versatile an item to lose. Wear it with a pair of jeans or even shorts, use it to top off a skimpy sweater dress or elegant silk separates: summer and winter alike, it always looks sharp and slick.

Sweaters are flexible and more comfortable to work in than a structured jacket. A crisp sweater, tastefully accessorized, is smart enough for most business occasions. This one in waffle-knit has the added fashion details of a gathered and puffed sleeve and leather-covered buttons on the shoulderline.

❝ **When in doubt wear black.** ❞

Jennifer d'Abo

Jennifer d'Abo, COMPANY CHAIRPERSON

OFFICE CHECKLIST

Dressing for business success is largely about being well-groomed so whatever you wear, remember the importance of VIP polish. Manicured hands, controlled hairstyles, slick but understated make-up, shiny shoes and unsnagged stocking are all signs of the executive mind.

● Don't underestimate the value of a white shirt: it will smarten anything.

● Dress in layers for over-heated or air conditioned offices: peel off or pile on.

● Avoid linen – you want to look capable and clued-up, not crumpled.

● Even in a heatwave don't dress for a day by the coast. If you look as though you're dressed for sunbathing, it gives the impression you're not concentrating.

● Don't over-accessorize in the office. Keep the glitter for later, when your workaday outfit goes out on the town.

● Wearing a different outfit every day is not a sign of being well-dressed.

● Business women *never* use plastic carrier bags.

Wardrobe stretchers are the timeless separates that truly earn their keep. Take these three easy pieces designed by Mulberry Company. The T-shaped top, soft buttoned-through skirt and relaxed white cotton jacket are all simply styled and free from the fussy and ultimately dateable details that give most clothes their built-in obsolescence.

Basic clothes are all about flexibility and nothing needs to be more flexible than a jacket. Unlike a coat, which is all-enveloping and all-concealing, a jacket does not make its impact as a solo act but must top off and look good over numerous different combinations.

It's not surprising then that jackets come in countless guises and styles from the simple blazer, hacking jacket and blouson through to battle and safari jackets, boleros, windcheaters, parkas and pea jackets (to name only a few). An informal jacket should give a lift to casual separates, not just add a warm layer. If you have played safe with the colour of your winter coat, why not splash out on a colourful all-purpose jacket?

Though jackets are known for their versatility, when you split a suit and use the top half with other items do check the proportions carefully. What looks like a harmonious outfit on the hanger can be a mis-matched mistake once it's on and you discover that the lengths and widths don't work together.

Jackets make great travellers and are far more comfortable to drive in than bulkier, longer coats. They are also a more suitable weight for air travel, whatever the weather outside. Jackets come into their own during the in-between seasons, spring and autumn, when it's usually too warm for a full-length coat but too chilly to discard the top layer altogether.

Obviously you want a style that suits your shape. As a rule cropped, bellhop styles suit only the slim, whether tall or short. In any case most of us choose to cover up our bottoms whenever possible and longer jackets are of course warmer. As a jacket is a topper, raglan or dolman sleeves are popular, so that a variety of sleeve shapes can be worn underneath.

If you are heavy-hipped, make sure that your jacket is long enough: a ¾- or even ⅞-length coat is often preferable to, say, a blouson that breaks at the body's widest point. Choose blazers only if they are long-lined, and avoid low-buttoning styles of jacket at all costs.

Wrap-over or belted styles will emphasize a large bust. A single or double-breasted jacket with a V neck and revers or a shawl collar is far more flattering. If you are top-heavy, select a jacket with fastenings that start below the bustline.

'Borrowed from the boys' jackets are in fact often the best. They're capacious, practical and warm, so why not buy one of his for yourself? Look at boys' tweed jackets, black tuxedo jackets (they look most chic if not too oversized) to wear during the day, or motorbike leathers.

In black leather a zippered and studded jacket has its origins on the back of a motorbike, but nowadays it has become the central ingredient of many girls' wardrobes.

A leather jacket in a shade to suit you (left) could be your most versatile buy. It will work as happily with trousers as skirts, can look tough with jeans, delicate with lace or elegant with the right accessories, and it suits both city and country styles.

It is hard-wearing – in fact it will improve with age – waterproof, warm and comfortable. But for all its practicalities there's no doubt that it's biggest attraction is its universal sex appeal.

There's nothing more basic than blue denim. Practical and classless, denim almost succeeded in becoming the uniform of the 70's. The austere chic-ness of the 80's makes it a little ill at ease in smarter, say office or business, environments but it is still unsurpassed for casual work and leisure wear.

The classic-cut jeans jacket (right) looks as good on a girl as a guy and simply doesn't date. Buy one a size or two on the large side and you'll have plenty of room to pile on the layers and look as if the jacket is only on loan.

73

If you live in the country, what you wear is perfectly simple. You wear country classics: clothes you have always worn and that have always kept you warm. These classics include sensible, hard-wearing and time-less garments like quilted waistcoats, flat caps, cotton and wool mix shirts, cable-knit sweaters and wellington boots.

For the newcomer or occasional visitor it is all too easy to look out of place. If you live exclusively in bright poster colours or deli-cate fabrics, you are sure to. But most city wardrobes can be adapted for the country.

Firstly, dress to keep warm. Even if it's warm indoors the winter winds can be far more penetrating than in a city. Thermal underwear is a must in winter.

Choose sweaters that work in layers and can be piled on or peeled off depending on the weather. Wear trousers that are hard-wearing and comfortable, or else culottes; team them with thick woollen tights or socks, flat boots or leather walking shoes. Outdoors add a tweed or oiled thornproof jacket, or a sheepskin or duffle coat.

This big, easy, herringbone overcoat by Mulberry is a stylish all-occasions coat, as happy in town as in the country.

A cable-knit waistcoat is part of the layered look to beat the draughts.

Golfing shoes are smart and comfortable. The wide heel is an asset when walking along uneven streets.

Denim is the only cloth that breaks the country camouflage code. It is tough, hard-wearing and has become enough of a classic in its own right to be totally acceptable. The die-hards still wear earthy toned cords and tweeds instead.

COUNTRY COLOURS
Country clothes are camouflage coloured. For traditional country pursuits like track-ing or shooting camouflage obviously makes sense, and country dwellers gener-ally like to blend in with the landscape whether or not their activities make this a requirement. Earth browns and muddy tans, clear fern greens and drab olives, stone, sand and rust are among the shades that make up the muted country colour spectrum.

In summer the principles of camouflage still apply. As bright flowers bloom, country girls reach for their fresh, pretty frocks. Flower-sprigged cotton and print dirndl skirts – the look that made Laura Ashley her fortune – are favourites, as are pastel separates: canvas or cotton drill jeans in ice cream shades worn with soft, floral shirts and simple T-shirts.

Soft Shetland, Fairisle or angora sweaters and kilts in heathery tartans, or wool dresses, corduroy smocks or suede skirts tone down what could be a tough masculine look.

A man's trilby not only adds dash, it keeps out the rain on wet windy walks.

The cosy cashmere muffler, a collectible in any wardrobe, is indispensable in a country one.

Borrow or buy a man's collarless shirt: its minimal simplicity will balance the rich mix of patterns, plaids and textures.

Hand-knit sweater from a 1930's design is knitted in rich earth colours. Its homespun feel is in keeping with country classics.

The hacking jacket is one of the Great British Classics, copied all around the world. Its cut is very slim and flattering. This jacket, for instance, is American designer Perry Ellis's interpretation.

A country skirt should be a dirndl, wide and full enough to climb stiles and fences in.

Thick, woolly tights or socks are essential. Country colours match easily.

Flat lace-up leather shoes are sturdy and sensible for walking; when it's not too muddy, they make a welcome change from the ubiquitous green wellies and look just as much the part.

As every little girl will agree there's nothing nicer than dressing up. And for grown-up girls it spells fine fabrics, face-framing hats, elegant heels, fancy gloves and a chance to pull out all the stops.

Dressing up for a formal occasion is a chance to honour a special event with a bit of an effort. We all know how we'd like to look – attractive, fashionable, a credit to ourselves as well as to our family and friends – but it can be a daunting prospect. The price we pay for the ease of our casual clothes is an uncertainty about formal attire.

The secret is simplicity. The essence of looking elegant and at ease on formal occasions is feeling comfortable in your clothes. Look at the two outfits here, both of which are strikingly, not deceptively, simple – there's not a tricky line or fiddly detail in sight. A fussy or cluttered appearance is invariably flustering and that is the last thing you want. So beware of complicated clothes that look stunning only when you are standing still; they can literally fall apart – with gaping joins, fly-away panels or a skirt that rides up – as soon as you move about.

The simpler the line of your outfit, the more opportunity you have to add your personal stamp with accessories. The fabric itself can spell elegance: for summer choose silk, linen, lace or crisp cotton and for winter velvet, silk or wool gabardine.

Teaming up good basics like a silk shirt, a blazer, a classic skirt and an understated straw hat is one smart solution, but hardly the most glamorous or inspiring. In fact everyday clothes are rarely dramatic enough for a special occasion and there's a lot to be said for investing in one special formal outfit to grace the grander aspects of your social calendar. Though it may prove expensive on your cost-per-wear scale it's well worth it for the satisfaction of knowing that you will look spectacularly just right.

The shapes are simple, familiar, unstructured and easy-to-wear, but it is the clever coordinating, reverse-out tulip print that lifts these linen-mix basics by Jaeger into the luxury 'dressed up' class.

Give a hat a veil, blossom or feather. Bind it in braid or wrap it in ribbon. Paint it, spray it or cut out its crown. But remember – when it comes to trimming a hat, Less is very definitely More.

A dress is always the easiest thing to wear. You put it on and forget it. This one by Nipon Boutique in navy and white is stunningly under-stated – a case of nautical inspiration, not matelot madness.

FINISHING TOUCHES

The good news is that accessories don't need to match any longer – and a hat in a totally contrasting colour can make a stri-king impact. If the special occasion in question means that you're going to be on your feet for most of the day, be sure that your feet can take your choice of shoes for this length of time.

Apart from the obvious occasions like a grand garden party there are no rules to say that you ever have to wear a hat. But now that hats are back in style, they're the surest way to add panache to any outfit.

But should you choose a large or small brim – or none at all? Very basically, a wide-brimmed, picture hat is graceful and ele-gant, smaller shapes are stylish but safe and tiny titfers lead in cheek and chic. The uninitiated may find a smaller hat less of a strain; you will feel more comfortable if you can't actually see the brim.

What suits you depends on you, your clothes style and your size. Always choose a special-occasions hat in context with the outfit, and check the proportions carefully to prevent any one part dwarfing the rest.

Don't forget gloves: they can be fun and a chic way to add punch with a contrast shade or a perfect match.

❛ **Practise wearing your hat. Do the washing up in it, get used to its movements, discover its best angle, its reaction to wind or jostle, and you'll wear it on the day with total confidence.** ❜

David Shilling, HAT DESIGNER

A dark coloured all-day-long dress made of jersey gets the evening treatment with an overload of jewellery. A veritable plumber's tool kit of bold necklaces, earrings and bangles ensures a distinct contrast between day and evening dressing.

Day to night, the basics stay the same and you simply swop the accessories. Ease on the huge, flashy diamanté ear-clips and step out of your sober business shirt into a silk blouse with a soft rever.

It's not an excuse to let your manicure lapse – but don't lacy gloves add a deliciously witty and very un-workaday touch?

Add sheer dottiness with bold black stockings sprinkled with spots. Perfect the evening elegance with spiky black stilettos.

Now that casual dressing has become a way of life, the dividing line between day and evening wear is blurred. We no longer keep separate wardrobes for day and night. A fine silk shirt originally bought for special dinners will also add class to a business suit and a pair of leather trousers that are a daytime friend will grace most evening occasions with equal elan.

The relaxing of fixed rules has made it much easier to go out for the evening straight from the office. A few discreet changes to mark the hour mean you can successfully travel through the entire day without major upheaval.

But there are times, especially if convenience isn't a factor, when we all like to make a special effort. Even then, simple separates and easy dresses cut to suit your shape are still the most versatile solution. Unless you have a lot of money to spend, or dressy evenings figure heavily in your calendar, they will pay much higher dividends than fancy frocks. Choose tactile, luxury fabrics like silk, satin, lace and velvet that all spell after-six glamour. Another appropriate fabric is matt jersey: a cliché of the 70's, it has grown into an 80's classic because its fluid quality ensures that it drapes flatteringly on all figures.

To accentuate night-time glamour, high-key accessories are indispensable — glossy pumps, high or low heeled with glitzy trims (look out for detachable bows or diamanté buckles), small patent, satin or velvet clutch bags, huge satin bows to dress up workaday hairstyles, sheer or fancy stockings and, most important of all, the biggest and best costume jewellery you can afford.

Grand pieces of jewellery may be expensive, but they can make or break a look. Remember that the stunning diamanté brooch that gives such a lift to your evening outfit will also work wonders pinned to your dark wool coat.

Second-hand clothes in nostalgic and often dramatic shapes make stunning and thrifty evening buys and you know you won't meet your double. At the top of the used-clothes market you'll find that period pieces bought at auction cost far less than their modern counterparts and at the bottom, rummage sale end, everything goes for a song.

The real attraction of antique or period clothes, apart from the thrill of the bargain, is the chance to buy the style, quality and workmanship of yesteryear. Not surprisingly, recent fashions have made anything white, frilly and lacy prohibitively expensive, but if your taste is more exotic than popular, a visit to an auction will be a feast.

Before you buy anything old, check for stains, tears and moth holes and judge sensibly the amount of life left in the fabric. Missing buttons are easily replaced by others from the correct period and grubby but beautiful lace takes well to dyes.

EVENING GLAMOUR FOR EVERY SHAPE

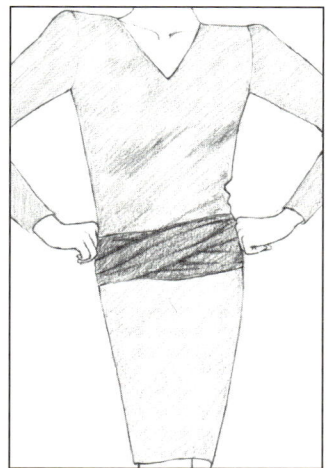

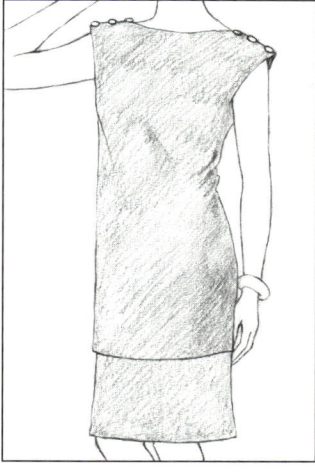

With a body-skimming, tapered dress which falls elegantly from padded shoulders – sashed on the hips and with a modest V neck – no-one will suspect that you have an over-large bust. Avoid elbow-length sleeves.

If you are very short, stick to stylish simplicity in a single colour (to include shoes and stockings). For evening this could be a tubular knee-length shift dress. Avoid ruffles, frills, high necklines and large patterns.

Use as many horizontal lines as possible to counteract the beanpole look if you are very tall. An off-the-shoulder neckline, wide cummerbund, change of colour and mid-calf length all foreshorten a silhouette.

Complement a wide hipline with easy, fluid separates. A long-line tunic top will give you a narrow, streamlined look and an extended neckline brings an illusion of added width to the shoulders.

THE LITTLE BLACK DRESS

Although the 'little black dress' has become something of a cliché, it is this century's one enduring fashion. It is that stunning number that always looks right and makes you feel good. It is the purest form of investment dressing and should never date from season to season. (If you can't wear black, read little navy, charcoal or even deep red dress.)

Its original concept was a dress that worked (with a change of accessories) for day or for evening. In ethnic or flamboyant phases, it can be overpowered, but it comes into its own when fashion calls for classics and right now is the item that no wardrobe should be without.

The beauty of the little black dress is its plainness. It is best cut into slim, sleek shapes and made in rich fabrics like silk, crepe or barathea. Its drama lies in its colour and simple styling allows it to take impressive chunks of jewellery for starry nights or a minimal gold chain for a simpler occasion.

The little black dress is one of the best second-hand buys. Check out your relatives' closets and charity shops for 1950's examples (the dress's last heyday), or even 1930's numbers if you are very lucky.

A V-necked velvet black dress (right) is given the glamour touch with diamanté and satin gloves.

Informal evenings may get more casual all the time, but grand evenings demand a specialized approach. If you attend a ball you should wear a ball dress and anyway it is worth investing in some definite after-dark clothes as much for personal morale as anything else.

If a ball dress really does make a mockery of your cost-per-wear scale, buy instead three easy but versatile pieces in a luxury fabric: matching camisole, bolero jacket and big, full-length skirt. Wear them all together for the special occasions, switch the skirt for a slimmer version or trousers for informal parties and wear the skirt with a silk blouse for black-tie dinners.

In many cases, short evening wear is sufficiently dressy, but never when the invitation states white tie for men. Ballerina-length (just above the ankles) can be charming, but is obviously only for those with well-turned ankles.

If you are big-busted and want to wear a revealing gown, choose a style with shoulder straps and sew a bra into the bodice. You can then forget about slipping straps.

Sleeveless gowns are very glamorous but not for those with flabby upper arms. This white voile blouse with see-through sleeves gives the bare effect without the cruel blatancy.

If fanciful fripperies or enchanting frocks are not your style, a man's tuxedo is a dramatic and viable alternative. The very young can wear a junk-shop find, but for more sophistication an excellent cut is vital.

If you choose to borrow verbatim and wear the wing-collar shirt and bow tie as well, remember to soften the effect with a feminine hairstyle and earrings. Vary your look with a silky camisole, glittery bandeau top, amusing brocade braces or satin shirt with a huge artist's bow.

EVENING OPTIONS

Many very large women feel that loose-shaped kaftans are their only alternative. In fact, they flatter nobody as they fall from the widest point and enlarge rather than disguise. If you do wear one, add a loosely tied sash at the hip, to give some shape and added interest. But preferably, aim instead to show off as much of your beautiful skin and shoulders as is attractive.

Nothing ruins the glamour of an evening outfit more than topping it off with just any old coat. You don't have to buy a special coat (although an antique evening coat always looks stunning). A fur is a good choice as it suits the richness of evening fabrics. And capes, shawls, ruanas – in fact any kind of wrap that does not have a definite hem length – prevent an orphan air.

Satin ballet shoes make exquisite and inexpensive slippers, and for those who like the height of heels it is a good idea to adapt a dressy pair of summer sandals.

Jewellery has always been a great ally, as it fills in bare expanses and hides ageing necks.

Give a black velvet choker an 80's touch by tying it in a bow and securing with a glittering diamond or paste brooch in a look popularized by Princess Michael of Kent.

As no one expects all pearls to come from oysters these days you can pile them on with impunity in a style that was worn by Queen Mary and has now found favour with the Princess of Wales.

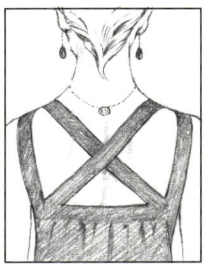

A backless gown may make a dramatic exit and crave an audience on the dance floor, but make sure that the interest is not all at the back for a sit-down dinner. What is stunning for the waiters is plain boring for your dinner companions across the table.

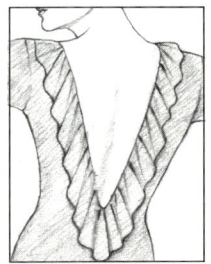

A criss-cross back shows off a beautiful nape and gives a pendant a surprising twist (top).

A backline that works well is a deep V, especially if it is mirrored by a plunge neckline as in the classic Bruce Oldfield shape (above).

Invest in a ball gown – it will save you anguish every time that grand occasion arises. Choose one that will serve for summer and winter and look wonderful for years, like this stunning black velvet and pink polka dot taffeta dress by Belville Sassoon.

DRESSING FOR YOUR LIFESTYLE

The type of holiday you book determines the kind of clothes you pack. Staying in a hotel demands a fairly formal wardrobe: cover-ups for breakfast and lunch, dressier outfits for evening. With self-catering you can be as relaxed as you choose, but for your own morale remember to take something more glamorous for evenings out.

If you are aiming to flop on the beach for two weeks with a bundle of books you won't need much more than beachwear and a couple of kangas. If, on the other hand, you plan to see the sights, you have to pack accordingly – depending on whether you'll be visiting ancient monuments, exploring the local countryside or sampling the night life.

Don't over-pack: friends will have less patience with a girl who can't manage her own suitcase than with one who wears the same outfit on several occasions. Travel in something comfortable that you will also wear during your vacation.

Holiday clothes are less affected by the dictates of fashion than our city wardrobes may be. The truly timeless garments like sundresses, shorts and camisoles are worth investing in. Even if you don't wear them much in a single year, you'll wear them every summer holiday for years to come.

KANGAS

This piece of cloth about 5 ft by 4 ft (1.5 m by 1.2 m) is an invaluable holiday wardrobe stretcher. It can be worn as a dress, a skirt, a pair of shorts or trousers, a strapless shift and a turban, as well as in its original western guise as a sarong or cover-up on the beach.

If your general wardrobe is fairly classic, holidays are a golden opportunity to break out of the mould and be more adventurous. Splash out with clothes that your job, or weather restrictions, simply would not permit at home.

If you are vacationing abroad, it can be fun to indulge in a more ethnic form of dress. This embroidered voile shirt and loose dhobi trousers make a lively all-purpose outfit. It is equally appropriate for the beach or, simply accessorized, at a table in a candle-lit restaurant.

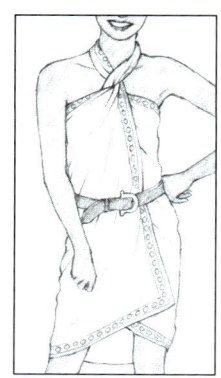

A kanga becomes a halter-necked dress if you twist the ends and tie round your neck. The dress needs only a chunky belt to hold it in place.

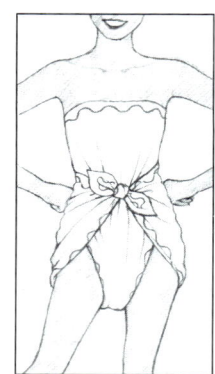

For a playsuit pull the bottom of the cloth through your legs, then bring it round and tie it in the front to make the 'bloomers'.

A sarong skirt is made by draping and tucking the kanga round your body. It looks equally good with a T-shirt or bikini.

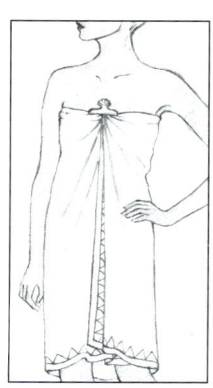

The simplest wrap of all — the sarong dress. Either tuck and knot the folds together or secure with a colourful hair peg.

Once you have acquired a warm, golden tan then flaunt it: choose clothes that expose your bronzed body to the maximum. But don't forget that you can still play the illusion game.

The dress (left) is perfect for the hippy girl. The black skirt has quite a slimming effect in contrast to the white of the bodice, but who would notice a broad beam with an enticing cut-away back to divert the eyes?

Remember that strap marks are unattractive, so plan your tanning with extra care for unusually cut dresses.

'Travel light' is always a good maxim, but particularly so if you are travelling by air or by train. Porters do not always appear when you need them and trolleys can be elusive. It is vital that you should be able to carry all your luggage without too much trouble, otherwise the holiday could get off to a bad start. Canvas or reinforced nylon weigh least and make remarkably durable luggage.

Before you pack, lay everything you could possibly want out on your bed and then eliminate individual articles as you group together a small wardrobe in which every item works hard. As you pack, make sure you include everything that each garment needs. Without, say, a backless bra or matching belt some tops will come home unworn.

Don't waste space: stuff shoes with cotton wool or socks, lay belts flat, not coiled, and decant beauty products into small unbreakable containers. Pack only the hair basics: remember extra conditioner for sun-bleached hair, but try and leave if not the hair drier at least the heated rollers at home. Covered elastics, ribbons and colourful slides make far better holiday hair accessories than lacquer and tongs.

Pack clothes flat or rolled, whichever suits your luggage. In general, holdalls take rolled clothes best while flat packing is most appropriate for cases. Very delicate fabrics like silk are generally better packed flat, but only if ample tissue is used on each layer. Rolling clothes eliminates marked creases and any crumples seem to fall out quickly. It also gives you maximum space.

If anything creases badly en route, hang it over the bath while you run a hot tub and all but the most stubborn creases will readily steam out.

Keep to a colour scheme like soft rose pink with a hint of beige. Versatile cotton separates – a long cardigan and brief shorts with forgiving elasticated waist – are matched up with flat espadrilles and pulled together with anything that is to hand – in this case a belt made from a length of string.

CHOOSE A COLOUR THEME

Simplify your final selection of clothes by sticking to a restricted colour scheme. Pick out versatile and favourite separates in, say, white and khaki with pink/navy/ yellow/ or black, or red and white with grey/acid green/ or tan. Run riot with one dress that is totally outside your colour palette to stop you feeling too controlled (but make sure you can wear your neutral shoes with it).

You can afford to be more adventurous with colour on holidays. Bright or intense shades look particularly good in the sunshine and you will find it easier to carry them off with a suntanned skin.

Necessity may force you to improvise and mix clothes more inventively than you would at home. Accessories will always add further variation: include several bright belts and some eye-catching jewellery to bring interest or glamour to simple clothes. The right amount of local colour can add a humorous dash, but do take care with ethnic local buys: the over-enthusiastic holiday shopper can appear ridiculous.

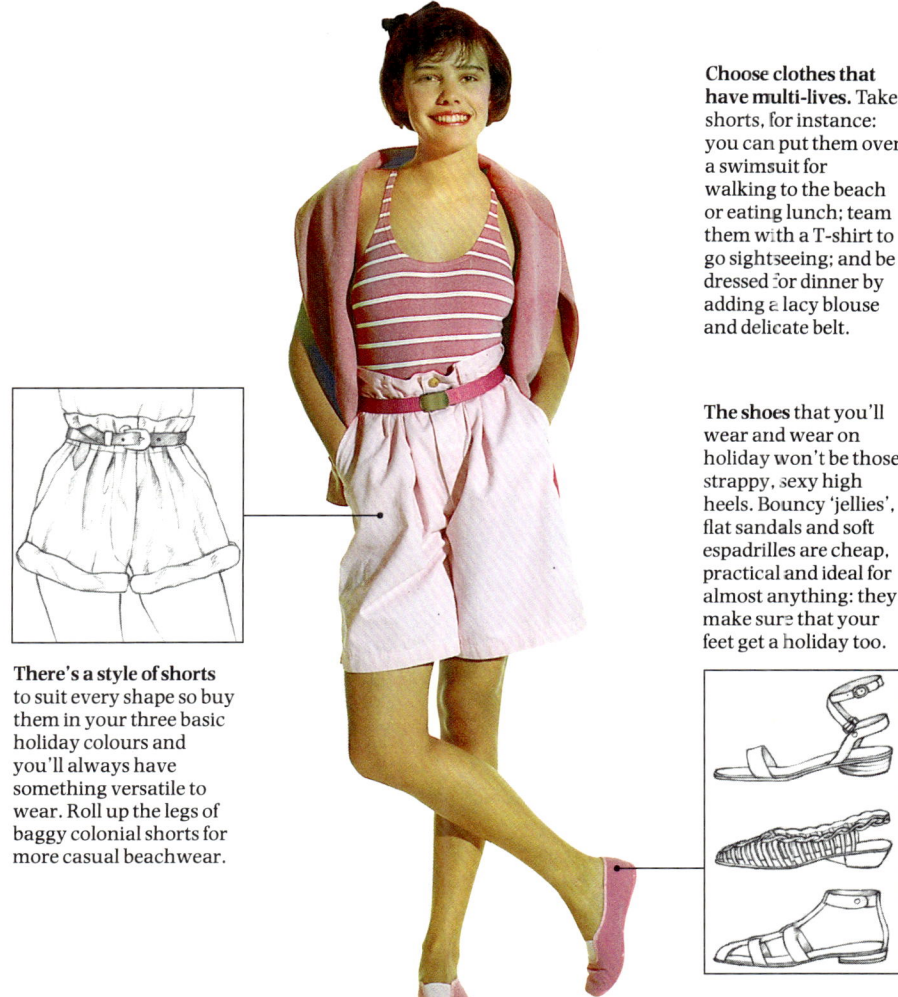

Choose clothes that have multi-lives. Take shorts, for instance: you can put them over a swimsuit for walking to the beach or eating lunch; team them with a T-shirt to go sightseeing; and be dressed for dinner by adding a lacy blouse and delicate belt.

The shoes that you'll wear and wear on holiday won't be those strappy, sexy high heels. Bouncy 'jellies', flat sandals and soft espadrilles are cheap, practical and ideal for almost anything: they make sure that your feet get a holiday too.

There's a style of shorts to suit every shape so buy them in your three basic holiday colours and you'll always have something versatile to wear. Roll up the legs of baggy colonial shorts for more casual beachwear.

BIKINIS FOR EVERY SHAPE

Most of the time we can hide or disguise the bits of our bodies we feel least happy about, but the beach or poolside bare-all leaves little room for manoeuvre.

Regardless of the swing-back towards one-piece suits and the increasing number of topless bathers, the bikini is still the most popular choice for beachwear. Choosing a bikini is no simple matter, as this brief garment comes in so many different permutations. Women with uneven proportions can now buy separate tops and bottoms.

Large ladies are advised to give this fashion a miss, unless their ample proportions are Junoesque rather than flabby. Trunks are not flattering, so if you have a very large bottom, stick to a one-piece swimsuit.

If you're very skinny, avoid anything totally strapless. Added frills or decoration help to make the most of a slender shape, as does a top which knots in the front.

Halter necklines suit pear-shaped figures as the inset straps give the illusion of width and thus balance to the shoulders. High-cut briefs avoid breaking the hipline at its widest point.

The heavy-busted do best to opt for light underwiring that offers support; choose a stretch fabric that will give and cover rather than cut into the bustline. Regular shoulder straps give the most support. Briefs can be minimal.

85

DRESSING FOR YOUR LIFESTYLE

Fitness, health and muscle are the buzz words of the 80's. Nowadays we are all good sports, whether we are training for a marathon or indulging in a bout of armchair chess. And we all love to dress for the active age: it is no accident that sweatshirts, ski jackets, running shorts, polo shirts, jazz shoes, legwarmers, leotards, cricket sweaters, tracksuits and sweatbands proliferate in the wardrobes of the least energetic.

Fashion designers were quick to recognize that even if we can't play the game we like to look the part and that we are loathe to relinquish the comfort and youthful spirit of sportswear. Accordingly they produced ranges of easy-care, easy-wear street clothes which, both in fabric and in shape, have their roots in the sportsfield.

And it is a two-way traffic. As soon as the fashion world put their money on sporty street clothes, active sportswear benefited from the designer stamp with fresher colour combinations, more figure-conscious shapes and slicker styling.

Jeff Banks' all-in-one playsuit made of sweatshirt material: easy, relaxed and not far removed from the locker room.

ON THE COURTS

You don't have to go to a specialist shop to buy your clothes for tennis or any other racket games. Fancy names and motifs emblazoned all over your body won't make you play any better. All you really need is a cotton T-shirt, comfortable shorts, socks and a pair of bumpers. But if you play a lot bear in mind that the clothes made by sports manufacturers are designed to give you unrestricted ease of movement and that proper tennis shoes will support your feet far better than sneakers.

Whether you choose to buy special tennis clothes or adapt your everyday wear, a natural fibre, especially cotton, is by far the most pleasant to play in and white is still the freshest colour. Now that other colours have become acceptable in all but the stuffiest of clubs, a splash of bright or pastel colour for accessories adds a witty touch.

Socks and stretchy belts come in many hues, as do wristbands and headbands, which serve a practical purpose in mopping up perspiration as well as looking suitably sporty.

A jogging suit is ideal clothing for winter play and for warming up in summer, but here again there is nothing wrong with adding an ordinary cardigan. A sleeveless waistcoat makes sense in cool weather as it will help to retain body heat without limiting movement.

As with all strenuous activities, wearing a sports bra gives support. Waist-high panties will prevent ugly gaps when your skirt blows up, or ridges if you choose shorts. Frilly knickers, invented back in 1949 for Gussie Moran by the irrepressible tennis clothes designer Teddy Tinling, are perennially popular under a skirt or dress and add a welcome feminine touch to what is now virtually a unisex kit.

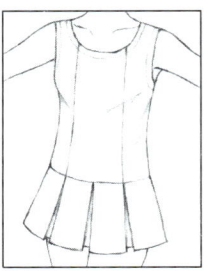

A structured long-line dress is ideal for larger players, especially older women, as this style usually comes in two lengths.

A culotte or divided skirt works well on most figure shapes – better than brief shorts, which make only the very slim look *gamin*.

Kilts have adjustable waists, suitable for those with a fluctuating waistline. They also flatten and slim the stomach, but the pleats tend to stick out over a big bottom.

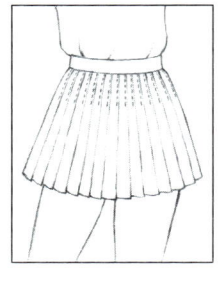

A skirt with stitched down pleats will sit flat and flatteringly over larger hiplines; avoid fancy panties underneath this style.

SOCKS TO SUIT YOUR LEGS

There are three distinct sorts of tennis sock and each, if you watch a top match, has its supporters. Bobble-back socks line the shoe (the bobble at the back is to keep the sock up), give a leggy look and will prevent a tidemark mid-calf if you plan to catch a tan while playing. Knee-high socks have seamless feet to eliminate rubbing – they look crisp with tailored shorts but are not for the petite as they cut the calf at its widest point. Most girls' favourite are ankle socks as they look the most feminine.

Whatever the style, opt for socks with enough natural absorbency and look out for specialist sports socks with a padded insole for cushioned support.

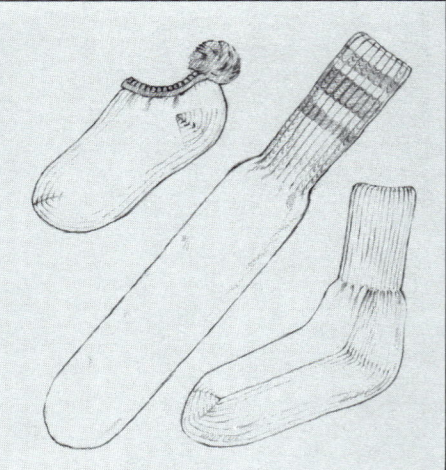

You will never play well if you are worrying about how you look, so fussy or difficult styles of dress are redundant.

Remember too to keep your hair out of your eyes. However attractive your hairstyle it will hinder your game if you continually have to fiddle with it. Experiment until you find a style that suits the sport. Headbands help to keep hair off the face. Pony tails and plaits are ideal for longer styles and slides will hold back stray wisps that could be annoying.

If you are invited yachting and don't know what to wear, ask yourself a few simple questions. Are you staying on a sailing boat or a motor boat? Will it be a smart or casual weekend? Are your friends serious or social sailors? Answer these and your kit bag (never take a hard-cornered case on a boat) will be sure to contain the right gear.

The only essential, without which most 'captains' will ban you from their boats, is a pair of flat rubber or rope-soled shoes. The social sailor need add little to her basic sporty wardrobe, so pack jeans, cotton drill trousers, warm, preferably oiled, sweaters, T-shirts, sweatshirts and a water- or wind-proofed jacket; add a swimsuit and you won't put a rubber-soled foot wrong.

Visibility is as important to the sailor as it is to the night cyclist. The colours of the yachting world, like those of the country, are regimented. Red, navy, white and yellow form the basis with splashes of bright blue and orange. Avoid totally the land-associated shades – green, brown and black.

What to wear to a smart yacht club depends on the time of day. Even at the most exclusive establishments the rules are fairly relaxed at lunchtime, though in the evenings the code can make the uninitiated feel uneasy.

Basically, stick to clear, bright colours and choose crisp, natural fibres. Cheat and look every inch the part by topping almost anything with a well-cut navy blazer or cotton blouson jacket. The social sailor can even get away with wearing white cotton trousers – and expect them to stay white for most of the day.

RACING SWIMSUITS

Today's racing suits are so stylish that they are worn by fashion-conscious swimmers and serious competitors alike. Their sleek, sporty lines flatter most body shapes and their technically advanced designs ensure maximum practicality. Deep armholes allow plenty of shoulder movement and a high-cut legline gives unequalled freedom as well as lengthening the legs and slenderizing the hips.

All racing suits should fit snugly, even tightly; if you have a large bust, look for elasticated support under the bustline. A keyhole back is a good choice for competition swimmers as it eliminates air pockets that form and fill with water during starts and turns, causing 'drag' on the body.

Goggles stop your eyes stinging when swimming in chlorinated pools. A swim cap is also a good idea as chlorine can damage your hair if you regularly go hatless.

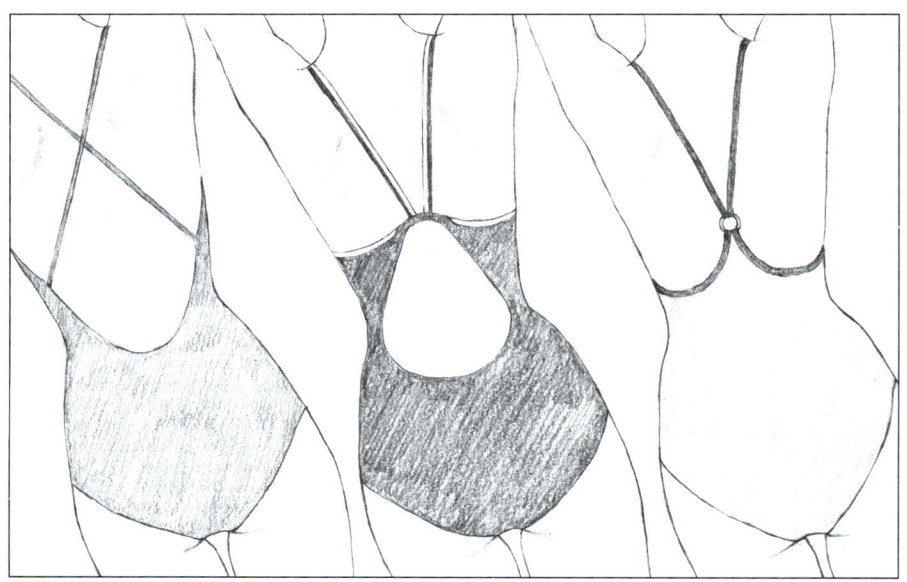

Serious yachtswomen
– those who participate as well as decorate – need heartier, practical clothes to ensure they stay warm and dry on the high seas. Cotton and wool underpinnings are a must; top them off with effective oilskins – those with efficient fasteners and cuffed ankles and wrists to keep out the wind and the wet.

A towelling scarf at the neck is absorbent, soft and warm and sailing boots with drawstring tops are far more weatherproof than regular sailing shoes.

All-in-one suits made from oilskin or nylon ciré are the driest for active wear and a suit or a jacket with a hood makes good sense.

The best skiing outfits are pared down to the bare essentials, with no superfluous or gimmicky details to mar the outline. The one-piece flying or boiler suit scores highest in every respect. It looks sleek, it gives the greatest ease of movement and does not allow snow to sneak in.

Always remember that skiwear must above all be warm and practical – choose a suit made from a strong waterproof fabric which also breathes, with an efficient lining like down or the less bulky one which works on the principle of conductive heat.

The stylish skier wears a headband, not a hat and sunglasses rather than goggles (unless weather conditions are extreme). She shuns extraneous bags on belts, bum bags tied round the waist, and certainly a rucksack. She stashes the basics of the day – such as tissues and lipsalve – into zip compartments or pockets on the legs, arms and chest of her suit (never around the hips or tummy).

If you need to, it is simple – and still chic – to add an extra layer with a gilet. A jacket with zip-out sleeves will give you a ready-made gilet to wear either on its own or as an extra layer over a one-piece suit.

The all-in-one suit is by far the most flattering of all the skiwear options for virtually every figure shape. This one is accentuated by big shoulders and a pulled-in waist.

Hats tend to make you overheat and are scorned by the stylish skier. Headbands or earmuffs are much more comfortable. Carry a beanie hat for bad conditions, but if your suit has a zip-out hood you already have the more practical alternative.

50's style ski-pants complete with stirrups under the foot are making a comeback on and off the slopes. Add a scarf wrapped round the head Audrey Hepburn style, and vivid pink lipstick to complete the 50's look.

Mitts are a boon for anyone with bad circulation but tend to be unwieldy and too hot for some skiers who prefer gloves.

If you hire your ski-boots and skis, have them fitted carefully. 'Moon' boots – insulated nylon boots with thick rubber soles – are the best footwear for apres-ski: anything else slips. Take a pair of cooler, lighter-weight shoes for restaurants.

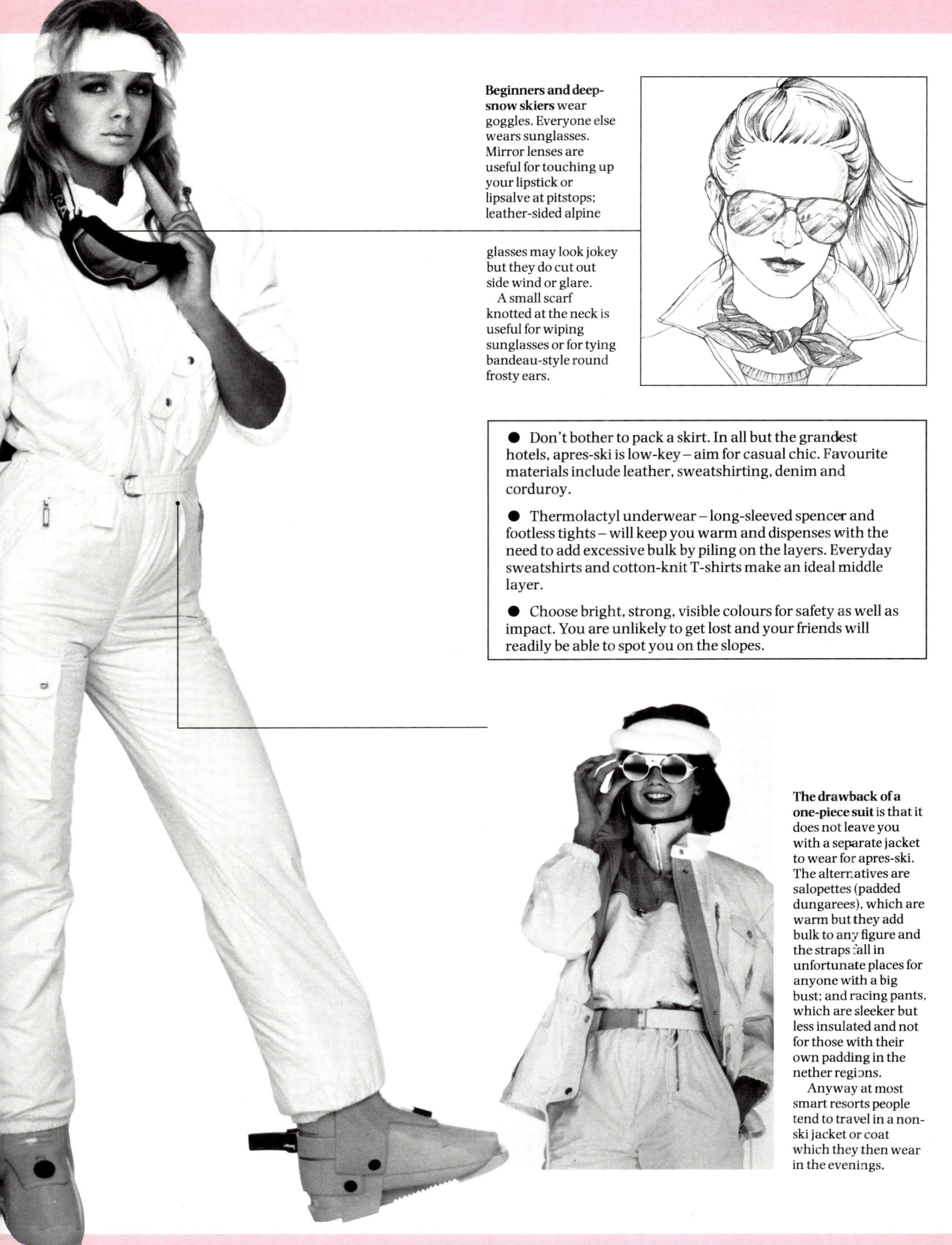

Beginners and deep-snow skiers wear goggles. Everyone else wears sunglasses. Mirror lenses are useful for touching up your lipstick or lipsalve at pitstops; leather-sided alpine glasses may look jokey but they do cut out side wind or glare.

A small scarf knotted at the neck is useful for wiping sunglasses or for tying bandeau-style round frosty ears.

● Don't bother to pack a skirt. In all but the grandest hotels, apres-ski is low-key – aim for casual chic. Favourite materials include leather, sweatshirting, denim and corduroy.

● Thermolactyl underwear – long-sleeved spencer and footless tights – will keep you warm and dispenses with the need to add excessive bulk by piling on the layers. Everyday sweatshirts and cotton-knit T-shirts make an ideal middle layer.

● Choose bright, strong, visible colours for safety as well as impact. You are unlikely to get lost and your friends will readily be able to spot you on the slopes.

The drawback of a one-piece suit is that it does not leave you with a separate jacket to wear for apres-ski. The alternatives are salopettes (padded dungarees), which are warm but they add bulk to any figure and the straps fall in unfortunate places for anyone with a big bust; and racing pants, which are sleeker but less insulated and not for those with their own padding in the nether regions.

Anyway at most smart resorts people tend to travel in a non-ski jacket or coat which they then wear in the evenings.

Aerobics, calisthenics or just plain keep fit, the fitness boom has introduced a whole new wardrobe to the dance studios and gymnasiums. Replacing the standard black costumes are leotards and tights in peacock colours and body-loving shapes.

Your body dictates what you can and cannot wear. As most of us have more curves than the model (right) and need to wear a bra for energetic exercise, her hori-zontal striped, U-backed leotard is unlikely to be the best choice of outfit – but we can all use the art of illusion to give us a helping shape-up.

Inset shoulder pads will slim down the entire body. Shiny black tights worn with a colourful, patterned leotard will minimize the thighs and diagonal stripes lengthen and slim the body as they contour the curves and disguise the bulges.

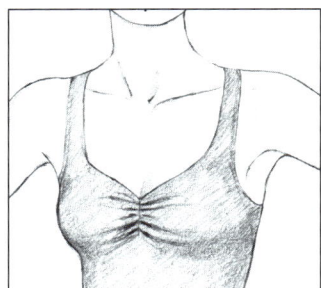

Leotards flatten the bustline, but you can put the curves back by re-shaping the front. Gather up the top 3in (8cm) in the centre of your leotard, then stitch a piece of lightly stretched elastic along the back to hold the ruching in place.

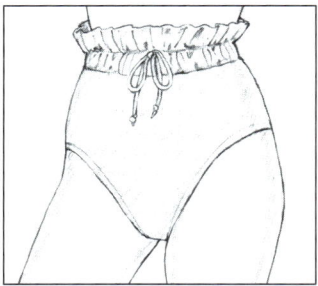

Dance knickers are the newest addition to the fitness fanatic's wardrobe. Wear them over a leotard or team them with a T-shirt or cropped top. They're a boon for the long-bodied who find that regular leotards cut into them.

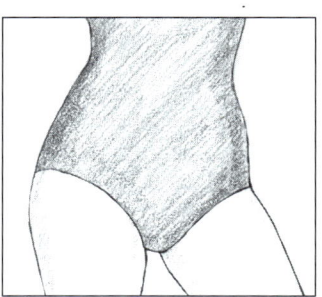

The high-cut legline (far right) lengthens legs and flatters all shapes. Don't pull it higher than the hipbone as that will broaden the beam. A lower-cut legline allows you to wear panties under your leotard. To avoid a pantie line, use liners.

❛ **Vanity is the number one reason for exercising (followed by health and sex), so it is vital for morale to look glamorous in class. It is too discouraging to stare at your reflection in the full-length mirrors around the studio if you are not dressed your best. Wearing terrific kit is all part of the healthy business of loving yourself.** ❜

Jackie Genova, FITNESS EXPERT

Authentic running clothes are essential to even the casual jogger. Fashion equivalents may look as though they will do the job, but you will discover (probably painfully) that their cut or fabric simply isn't suitable.

Runners expend a great deal of energy and tend to perspire, so they must wear clothes designed to cope with this excess moisture. Pure cotton is not suitable as it tends to get soggy, clammy and to lose its shape. Vests with a synthetic mesh panel are not only cooler, but also dry off more quickly.

The best all-weather suits are made of a fabric that breathes – its billions of tiny pores allow sweat vapour to escape while keeping rain and wind out. You can work your body hard and still stay warm and dry.

Never buy running shoes on looks alone. They need to be tailored to your specific requirements, so it is always worth seeking specialist help.

SPORTS BRAS

Sports bras are specially designed to help you play any sport in comfort by eliminating slide and pressure points. The best ones are made in moisture-regulating cotton and lycra.

Their seamless cups, adjustable, grip-fastening straps and padded front fastening all help to stop rubbing. This model by Triumph also has a functionally styled back to give full freedom of movement; the position of the straps prevents them slipping off the shoulder.

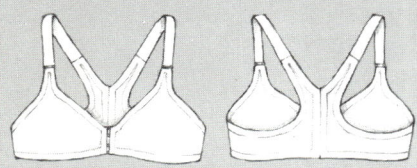

Wear a sleeveless vest with low-cut armholes to stop chafing and with seams that won't rub. For running in hot weather choose shorts made of lightweight nylon as it helps to stop overheating.

Grey is again a favourite colour for jogging suits. A sweatshirt top is the most comfortable option; make sure it is generous enough to lap well over the trousers. Ensure that the legs are slim enough not to flap when you run.

❛ I think I've got big legs so I steer clear of long shorts and always choose minimal shapes with high-cut leotard-style legs. And I like vests with V-necks which flatter my broad shoulders. I design tracksuits and always add shoulder pads to give an Armani-type line. The spectator can't tell where my shoulders end and the suit begins. ❜

Leslie Watson

Leslie Watson, MARATHON RUNNER

93

The biggest mistake you can make is to regard maternity wear with a make-do-and-mend attitude. A pregnancy may only last a few months but this is no reason to scrimp over the clothes you will have to wear day in and day out. The chances are that you may have a second pregnancy and, far more important, this is supposed to be a joyous and happy time of your life. Your body will go through such a dramatic change that you are sure to need the comfort and security of good, well-cut and above all attractive clothes.

As soon as you discover you are pregnant, plan a strategy. Do you want to advertise or minimize the fact? Consider both your feelings and the suitability to your work surroundings. About half the maternity wear is designed to disguise the burgeoning bump, the other half styled to announce the arrival loud and clear.

The detractors work on the principle that by accentuating the slim bits of your body – legs, neck and hips – you can divert attention away from the stomach. A broad-shouldered tunic is unbeatable, especially if it has added shoulder pads. It will skim the body gracefully and cinch in at the hipline. Tunics can be worn with long or short skirts as well as trousers and will keep most onlookers in the dark for many months.

A man's borrowed, long-line sweater is another disguise. Wear one over your regular jeans, simply leaving the jeans zip undone and clip on a pair of braces to keep them up.

Artfully-cut A-line dresses are ideal for the small busted, but as most pregnant women's breasts increase considerably they can simply hang from the bust in an uncompromising tent.

The pinafore is the most versatile buy. You can pop a pinafore over almost anything and normal shirts can be worn right through pregnancy as no one will see that the buttons are left undone. A pinafore can be made in durable cord or canvas for day and velvet or stiff silk for night.

Among the advertisers, dungarees or all-in-one playsuits with added front fabric are sporty, but they leave nothing to the imagination. Wearing a hip belt is a recent innovation in line with contemporary fashion trends – it pronounces the pregnancy but does give a pulled-together outline.

It is perfectly possible to get by without specialized purchases. Choose garments that are not only broad across the beam, but that also have roomy armholes and adjustable waists and fastenings. Don't forget to even up the hemlines as your pregnancy progresses.

Natural fibres are every mother-to-be's best friend: they help to keep you cool when your temperature rises as well as the weather's. Sleeveless tops and dresses in lightweight cotton are best in the summer. Loose, drawstring-waisted culottes have a sporty look and a sunhat will stop you feeling flustered.

Get away from regular, tent-shaped dresses with a flatteringly cut smock. The wool dress (left) has a bib front which fits flat over the bustline, and gathers which open gently to accommodate the bump.

Be a stunning lady-in-waiting in bright, eye-catching clothes. This tunic, worn with cropped trousers, is cut wide to balance the pregnant shape.

Accessories are the one part of your wardrobe you don't have to pack away when pregnant. Be brave with jewellery, scarves and shawls. Draw the line upwards with extravagant ear-clips, or down to a neat ankle with interesting stockings.

Carry a small, neat clutch bag. With the extra bulk you are already carrying around, a bulging saddlebag will not only make you feel like a pack-horse – you could look like one too.

A wrap around cover-up will keep you smart and warm with no gaping buttonholes or straining fabrics.

Flat shoes are obviously the most comfortable though you can sport high heels for short periods on special occasions. On a daily basis, choose heels from flat to a maximum $2\frac{1}{2}$ inches (60 mm). And note that 80 per cent of women's feet elongate during pregnancy, so take care not to cause corns or callouses from wearing over-tight shoes.

Boost a sagging morale with pretty fashion touches. Interesting necklines like a blouse tied with a pussy-cat bow will detract attention from the bump.

A lacy collar added to a smock will make you feel fresh and feminine.

● Wrap up in a poncho or shawl: a coat left unbuttoned simply looks messy.

● You won't need maternity tights until the last two months. Until then, wear a larger size of normal tights the other way around.

● Choose a skirt with an elasticated U-shaped panel, to give your bottom half a slim outline.

● Spoil yourself – you may not be feeling very pretty so give yourself regular beauty treats like facials and manicures. You'll want a professional pedicure towards the end too, as you won't be able to reach your feet comfortably.

USING COLOUR

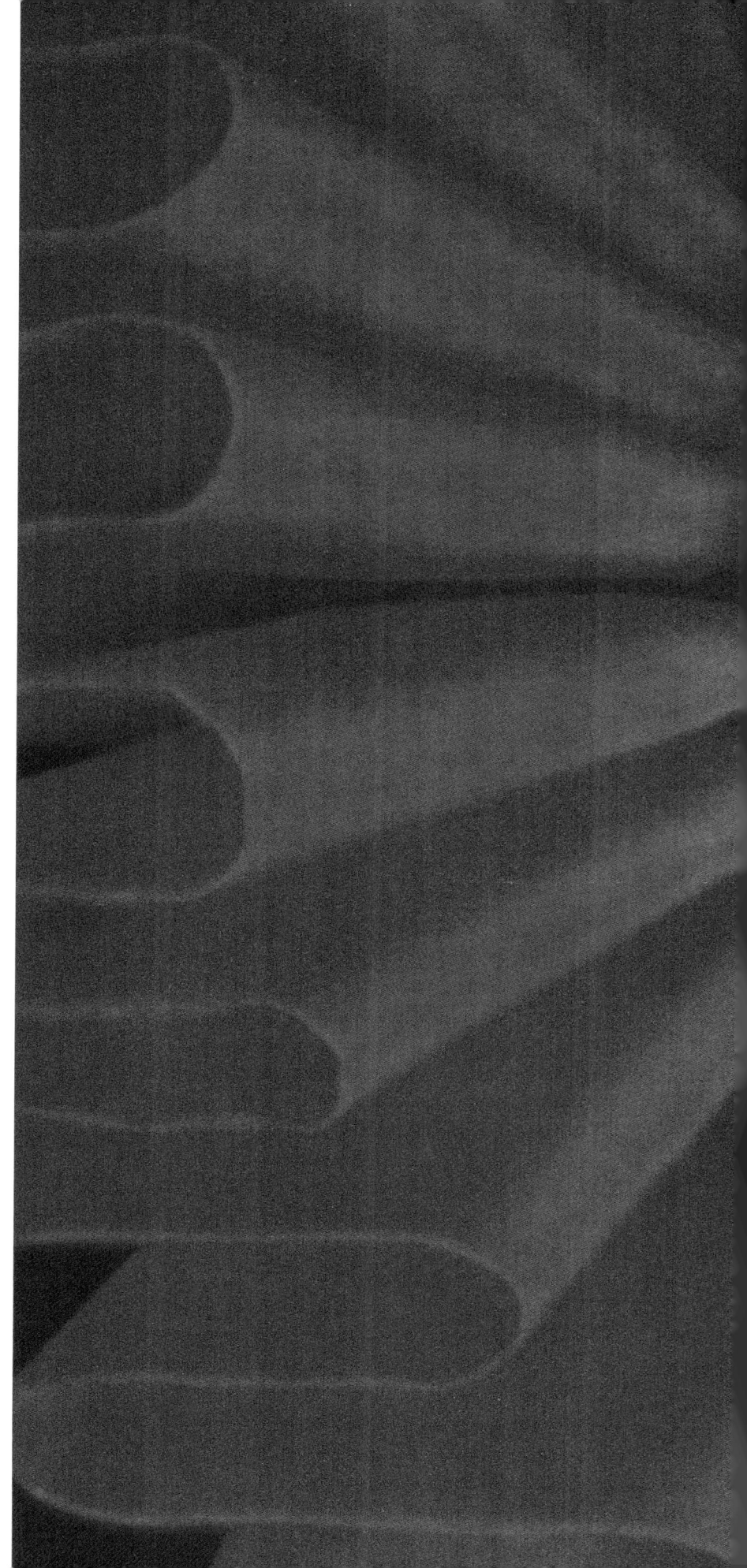

Colour is your wardrobe's best friend. Be bold and brave and mix your palette with abandon. Paint with the brights for razzmatazz, add subtlety with pastels, use neutrals for tone-on-tone texture and never underestimate the drama of black and white.

USING COLOUR

Just as you would choose an outfit to complement your colouring, so should you invest in make-up shades that flatter and enhance your basic skin tone. In other words, learn to turn your natural colouring to your advantage. Mastering the natural look means studying your skin tone, face shape and individual features in detail, in order to decide which make-up products will work best for you.

Everyone of us has a unique colouring determined by the blue or golden undertones of our skin, hair and eyes. According to one colour and wardrobe coordination theory, the secret to finding your best colours lies in nature's seasons. Each season has its characteristic colours and your colouring can be seen to harmonize with one of them. Whether your skin is yellow-based, pink-based, orange-based or olive-based classes you as 'late spring', 'very early summer' or whatever. However, as the distinctions are very fine and subtle, this type of analysis is best done by a colour consultant specially trained in this field.

An important rule is never to try to change your skin tone completely. The illusions make-up offers you are subtle ones, not complete changes of colouring and character. The main aim of effective foundation, or base colour, is to enhance your complexion and camouflage its less attractive characteristics. So when choosing foundation, test out a little on the inside of your wrist or along the back of your thumb bone and check the tones in daylight. Or rub a little into your jawline to find a shade which matches your skin tone. If you feel your natural colouring needs warming up or toning down, choose a slightly darker or a slightly lighter foundation in the same tonal range.

Catherine Deneuve, actress, has a cool, fair complexion. Your hair colour is often a clue to your own skin tone. If you are blonde, then your skin is probably fresh and fair, cream or light olive. Fair-skinned blondes run the risk of turning a whiter shade of pale, so foundation should have a warm, creamy tone, not pinky-white which will look unnatural.

Isabelle Huppert, actress, has red hair, freckles and a pink complexion. Redheads usually have either a pink or an ivory skin tone. Avoid shades that are tinged with pink and use a light-coverage foundation or a slightly tinted moisturizer for the best effect.

SKIN TONES

Skin is immensely variable in colour but it can be broken down into the following main groups according to its basic tone.

Ivory No skin tone is absolutely white, but ivory best describes very pale, translucent skin. To enhance this skin tone, match your foundation exactly. If you have true ivory colouring, your hair colour is likely to be either black, dark brown or auburn.

Cream The typical 'English Rose' complexion is a light, slightly peachy-beige skin tone. Your foundation shade can either match or verge slightly towards either side of the spectrum, a fraction lighter or darker.

Fair A delicate blush-like tone that tends to go with blonde hair. Match your foundation shade exactly.

Pink If you have red hair or freckles, more often than not you will have this 'rosy' skin tone that can become ruddy. Tone it down with a beige foundation, which has no pink undertones.

Olive The olive skin tone is usually associated with dark hair and dark brown eyes. Blondes with brown eyes often have olive skin, too, but it tends to be a lighter shade. As olive skin has a tendency to look sallow, especially in winter, it is best camouflaged with a slightly pink foundation. Otherwise, enhance it with exactly the same shade.

Brown Brown skin can range in shade from a suntanned complexion to a light coffee or very dark brown. Match your foundation to the precise skin tone. Avoid tan or bronze shades with a pink or brick-orange pigment.

Black There is no absolutely black skin tone, just as there is no absolutely white one. Though black-skinned girls don't necessarily need to wear foundation, there are base shades available in make-up ranges specifically designed for black skins.

❝ Some cosmetic ingredients can turn dark skins grey, others can turn them an unnatural red or yellow. But as black women have a natural bronze note to their skin they don't really need foundation except to cover blemishes or use under eyes.

You don't want anything that will change your skin colour so choose a base close to your own skin tone or use a bronzer. ❞

Beverly Johnson
TOP MODEL

Clio Goldsmith, former top model and now an actress, has a light olive complexion. If you have brown hair, then your skin tone is likely to be cream or olive. Choose a warm, biscuity-beige foundation for a healthy look, and warm up sallow skin with a slightly pink foundation.

Beverly Johnson, top American model, has a very dark brown complexion. If you are black-haired, then your skin tone is likely to be ivory, brown or black. Dark-skinned girls must wear exactly-matched foundation: if necessary, mix two together. For extra glow add a few drops of bronzing gel to your foundation.

99

Wearing make-up is the age-old art of illusion. It has a power to change not only your looks, but the way you feel and even your personality. Through the clever use of foundation, powder, blusher, shaders, highlighters and eyeshadows, you can create a look that you feel is right for you. A subtly made-up face can not only make you look beautiful, it can also give you a great psychological boost.

Correctly applied, make-up will enhance your good features and mask your bad ones – minimize a heavy jaw, for example, or cover up the odd blotch. Subtle camouflage apart, you should never try to alter your looks totally. Make-up is no longer intended to be obviously artificial. Today's products are lighter and smoother than they used to be and it is important that you should feel comfortable wearing them.

Vary your make-up colours according to the clothes you are wearing, and keep in step with changing fashions in cosmetics.

Never get into a rut with the same old colours applied in exactly the same way – otherwise you will date your face. Try out new colours and different shaping: part of the fun of using make-up is to experiment.

Before applying any cosmetics, it's important to recognize the overall shape of your face – be it oval, square, round or heart-shaped – and become familiar with your individual features. Once you decide which features you want to tone down and which to emphasize, then you can work out how to use make-up products effectively.

Remember that it makes sense to apply your cosmetics in the type of light you will be in when you are wearing them. Daytime make-up is best applied in natural light but for an evening look it is preferable to use an electric light. In either case make sure the light falls squarely on your face.

Never be afraid of make-up. There really are very few rules to follow. Apart from working out your complexion colouring and choosing the appropriate foundation shade (see previous page), there is a huge spectrum of colours to choose from in your tonal range. Just because you have blue eyes, it doesn't mean you have to wear blue eyeshadow. In fact, a contrasting shade may make your eyes look bluer than ever.

The art of clever make-up lies in the blending of colours, so invest in good make-up tools that you find easy to work with and blend, blend and blend again. This will enable you to create all sorts of shades that you might never have thought of wearing.

Apply blusher to warm up your looks and soften your bad features. Brush it not just on your cheeks but on your temples, browbones and chin, too. Use highlighter where you want to play up your good points. Be bold and adventurous when it comes to applying your blended shades of eyeshadow and lipstick: consider yourself an artist and work freely and imaginatively on your canvas.

Sophisticated dazzlers
Pinks, plums and mink shades can all combine to give a healthy sparkle to olive skins and suntanned faces. For intensity, rim the natural shape of your eyes on the upper and lower lids close to the lashline with a russet-brown pencil, or rim along the inner lower lid, as with khol. Brush lashes with brown mascara, and colour lips with a hint of coral.

COLOUR CHANGES

Take the varying seasons of the year into account when choosing make-up, and modify its style and its colouring accordingly.

In autumn and in winter add brightness to those grey days. Your skin will be paler and more sallow, so go for warm cheek tones and apply deeper eyeshadow colours, with bright, cheerful lipstick shades. In spring and summer, change your foundation to a light, slightly cooler shade, or just use a tinted moisturizer. Then have fun trying out the new season's make-up colours. A cool colour scheme works best in strong sunlight, so opt for pastels and more muted tones.

A change of hair colour will probably mean varying your make-up too. If the colour change is drastic, you may have to alter your wardrobe as well.

Green with envy For night-time glamour or to brighten up dull, wintry days, a mixture of green, yellow and russet works well on ivory complexions.

Use several shades for the eyes, blending carefully, and brush colour under lower lashes for intensity.

In the pink Pretty pinks are perfect for flattering most complexions as they give a light, warm glow. Brush them on just cheeks or browbones, or on lids and lips too for a luminous effect. If you use pink near the eyes, make sure the whites of your eyes are white and clear, otherwise the pink will only accentuate the effect of slightly bloodshot eyes.

Choose a pale pink to highlight browbones, darker pink in the socket lines and on lids to add depth. A pale pink will emphasize lips and make them appear fuller, while a darker pink will give the illusion of a smaller mouth.

USING COLOUR

Whether you play safe or go for daring permutations, there's only one rule with colour – once you've decided on your scheme, be it for your whole wardrobe or just for one day, wear it with confidence.

Carry the colour of your outfit through to your face to make for a more harmonious look. Today make-up knows no barriers, in terms of colour or where to apply it, so the possibilities are endless. You can add warmth to your face when wearing cold or muted winter shades – or go to the other extreme with a one-tone look. If you're confident enough to wear bold, bright shades, then strike out with make-up that inspires.

Cap it all – carry your colour coordination from top to toe.

Team your eyeshadows to a part of your outfit – in this case, a mixture of browns and yellows for eyes. Coordinate further with a tawny blusher, perfect for offsetting a pale winter complexion. Pink lips add a final touch of warmth and make for an altogether healthier glow.

Frame your face with colour. If you are young enough to get away with traffic-stopping shades, why not mix as many as possible near your face – they are sure to stop the focus from wandering.

The art of wearing unusual or vibrant colours lies in the blending. Don't be afraid of colour clashes, such as a mix of orange and pink shades for eyes. Give your look a lift with pearlized pink lips.

Subtle colour mixes – cigar, bitter chocolate, winter white and greige – get an added lift from a dash of lemon.

Darkest-chocolate- shaded gloves and bag make for accessories that will complement countless colour schemes.

Add interest to such a simple colour combination with contrasting textures.

Turn a striking outfit into a sensational one with a vibrant palette. Here an unavoidable orange combines with hot pink, lurid lime and startling lemon. One vest in a pattern of colours is great, but layering three in different hues certainly gives an interesting edge.

A total pastel make-up can make you appear wishy-washy, so opt instead for a clever mixture of light and dark. Brush lids in charcoal grey then highlight browbones with yellow – or whatever colour matches your pastel outfit. If your lips are well-shaped, keep them sweet in a pretty light pink shade.

If you're feeling out in the cold, make yourself the centre of attraction by going for a one-tone look. Then defy convention by applying the colour to eyebrows too. A positively pale complexion makes your chosen colour theme even more striking. Here the blue mood is given just a hint of warmth by applying a dash of pink on the browbones.

Pastel shades are a stunning choice for evening wear. You're sure to stand out from the crowd, especially in winter when many women rely on black.

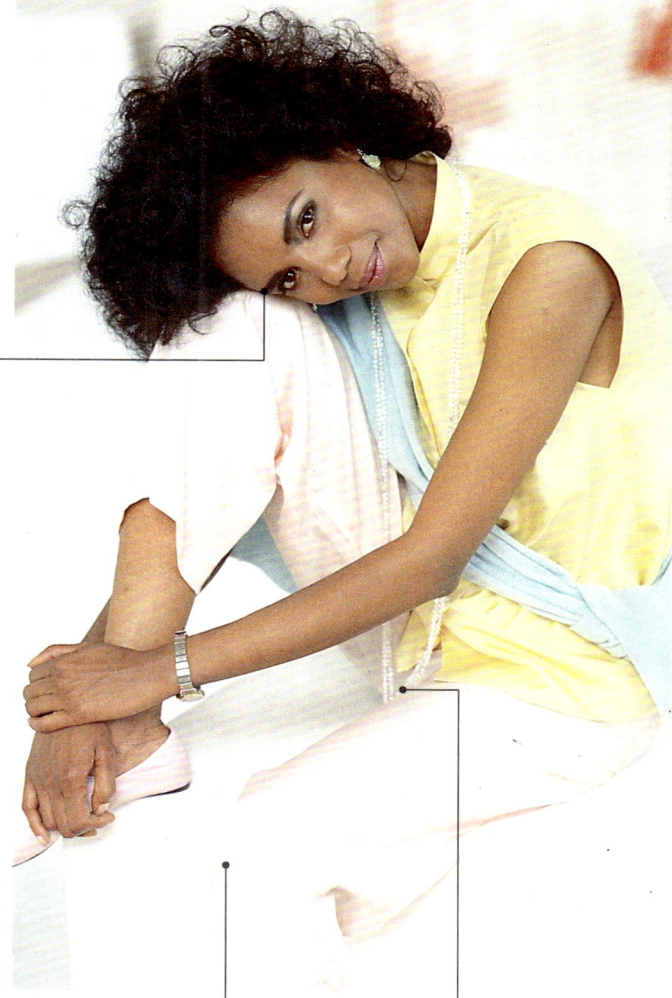

Blue, blue and more blue – a single colour theme need not look at all simple. It's not what you wear, but how you wear it. This outfit may appear bizarre, but check out the ingredients – they could hardly be simpler: a cap topping off a simple scarf, classic sweater and tracksuit trousers.

Pistachio, lemon and strawberry, the soft ice-cream shades don't have to be sickly sweet. Juxtapose these baby colours with sophisticated shapes for a chic but youthful style.

Don't coordinate pastel colour with matching jewellery – it looks far too contrived. Instead rely on crystal, that reflects colour and light, and the cool calmness of steel and gold.

Relief – a stripe of white for a splash of light.

The first thing you notice about a woman's clothes is their colour. The colours she chooses to wear or combine are the statement she makes about herself.

Many factors govern the colours we choose, and the most important – our colouring – hardly gets a look in amid myriad emotions, prejudices, insecurities and a desire to stand out from the crowd. We can also use colour to highlight our personality or, occasionally, confuse it. But it is rare to find a moody person decked out in sunshine yellow or a shy one dressed in shocking pink.

Our notions about the colours that suit us are not always accurate. We may dismiss our best colours – say, the detested colour of an old school uniform or green because of superstition. And if a husband or close friend loathes a certain shade we are unlikely to wear it, even if by doing so we would bring out our best features.

Colours traditionally link up with political beliefs, status or class: take revolutionary red, bohemian black or white collar workers – but this may or may not be a factor in the colours we choose to wear.

Colour analysts stress that the colours we select are an important indication of both mood and character. Red is related to sex and aggression, dominance and energy. It reveals impulsiveness and a desire to succeed – in love or in life.

Brown indicates a nature that seeks emotional security before sexual contentment. Blue points to a more tranquil and reserved character, yet one with high ideals and ambitions. Green suggests a nature that is egotistical and proud, that wants to impress, but is afraid to give way for fear of losing control.

Those who choose yellow are generally optimistic and sympathetic, without too many sexual hang-ups. Black indicates a stubborn character, likely to fly in the face of fate; one that is often out of step with others and feels misunderstood. Grey suggests one who stands on the sidelines and remains emotionally uncommitted.

But the choice of colour in clothes cannot be that cut and dried. Apart from our own need and desire for change, fashion is the major influence in changing the colours in our closets. Contrary to popular belief, drastic changes of colour are rare, and the introduction of new shades is nothing like as frequent as we all imagine.

Colour trends can cloud our instinctive desire for a shade we know is flattering, and also put it so out of favour that, even if we wanted to wear it, it would be difficult to buy. Take the case of brown and purple. Feted as the signature colours of the 60's, they were then shunned by the fashionably chic for well over ten years and have only recently re-emerged as colours that we want to wear. But as with everything that returns to fashion, it never reappears in quite the same shade or shapes as before.

It is difficult – without clinging to neutrals – to ignore fashion shades, because they dominate the choice in the stores, but wearing colours that don't work for you casts you in the role of fashion victim.

Go for interpretation rather than blind conformity. There's no point wearing a sweater in a fashionable shade of yellow if it makes you look jaundiced. The trick is to acknowledge the season's shades with an accessory, say yellow shoes, or make a bridge of colour between your skin and the popular but unflattering shade. Grey, for instance, drains the colour from most faces and, worn monochromatically, is drab and dreary – but add a dash of spice with a crimson neckerchief or cobalt blue beads and it becomes a classically kind neutral.

The colour wheel

Red, yellow and blue are the pure, primary colours from which every other colour is derived. They form the hub of the wheel, together with the colours obtained by mixing together these primaries. Yellow and red together make orange; yellow and blue produce green; and blue and red combined becomes purple.

The second ring shows what happens when 50 per cent white is added to the pure colours and the third ring displays the effect of an equal addition of black. The colour wheel shows us which families of colours harmonize (those that are adjacent on the wheel) and which contrast (those that are diagonally opposite)

as well as which are warm and which are cool.

The warm colours – reds, oranges and yellows – are opposite the cool ones – blues, greens and violets. And it's worth noting when we are choosing shades to wear that warm colours advance and cool colours recede.

The colours we choose to wear provoke a reaction in others. Looking at different colours alters our blood pressure, heartbeat and rate of respiration. Warm colours cause them to rise, preparing us to take sudden physical action, whereas cool colours induce a reduction.

COLOUR COMBINATIONS

Dressing by the colour wheel is dressing by the book. It is attractive, flattering and safe but, above all, limiting. Our wheel shows 36 different shades, but in reality the human eye can distinguish some 10 million variations. So it's up to you to add flair to your dress with an adventurous approach to colour combinations.

Colour is the best way to express your individuality – because your own colouring comes into the formula, the colours you choose to combine are unique to you. But you can also experiment with colours to produce unexpected but happy results.

Instinct can often be a better guide than colour theory, creating glorious mixed marriages. Right, a fuchsia silk shirt tops a burgundy silk vest and red suede wrap skirt – a case of achieving stunning effect by being bold with colour combinations.

105

USING COLOUR

It's perfectly possible to put together a successful wardrobe working to a restricted colour palette. Internationally acclaimed designer Jean Muir decided long ago that navy was her favourite colour and she would never wear anything else. But unless you are tremendously disciplined, a little variety goes a long way towards helping you to enjoy your clothes more.

A simple colour scheme can be a monochromatic one. You can choose various shades of the same colour – powder to cornflower to navy blue, for instance – or aim for harmonizing colours from adjacent sections of the wheel, for example lime green, dark holly green and turquoise

blue/green or various different pinks.

Once you feel a little more confident about colour you can create your own combinations. The easiest way to discover new possibilities is with a scrap bag. Collect together in a bag as many small cuttings of plain coloured fabric as possible. Pick out two pieces at random (if they look awful together, the experiment becomes even more interesting). Tip the rest of the scraps out of the bag then, holding the original combination together, place them against other colours. You will see how certain shades react together and may be surprised to find that, with the addition of one or more colours (often in varying propor-

tions), any combination, however unlikely, can be made to work.

Stir the cuttings round and see the wonderful colour combinations you can create purely by chance. This is how colour consultants and textile designers work to produce their felicitous partnerships each new season.

Now use your cuttings to try and establish your own best colours. By holding each scrap up to your face you will find that some colours make you look pale, flustered or drab, while others make your skin, eyes and hair spring into life. Look for shades of various colours that work well, rather than an actual hue. Most people can in fact wear 90 per cent of colours – it's the shade and intensity that determines whether a colour flatters you or not. Don't choose on skin tones alone – your hair, eyes, lips and teeth all come into the equation.

This selection can be a complicated procedure. Some colour consultants start by dividing all women into one of four 'seasonal' colour groups. You may need to ask a friend to help you choose, but in the end you should dicover some shades that are obviously your best colours. Try to favour them when you are choosing make-up colours as well as clothes, and attempt to wear them round your face for focus.

Dark emerald green, fuchsia and cobalt blue make for quite a heady combination. You have to work hard to pull it off, as colour matching in these strong shades has to be accurate to be successful.

106

- Warm, bright colours increase height, while subtle colours make the small look smaller.

- A change of colour at the waistline can cut a small person in half.

- A very loud, patterned shirt needs to be worn with strong, vibrant colours or the shock will ruin the effect.

- If you are dressing for the board room, spice up a navy or grey suit with a sweater, shirt, jacket, stockings or accessories in bright colours. Women don't need to dress invisibly any more to get on in business.

- Continually reassess your best colours. Natural colouring changes with age and a woman may find that her favourite shades start to look hard or dull while others, that were previously difficult to wear, suit her better.

- Most people know that appearing on television puts five pounds on them, but do you know the best colours for the box? White is too stark, black always drab, blue is cold and yellow can be distracting. Pale neutrals – tan, grey, peach and pink – are your best bet. Navy, red and green are acceptable too.

To achieve a basic wardrobe that works, keep to a colour theme – navy, grey, black or beige are the accepted basic neutrals to build on, but there is nothing to stop you choosing grass green or electric blue as your mainstay. All you have to bear in mind is that it will become more difficult to match these up in seasons when your chosen shade disappears from the fashion spectrum.

Like the chameleon, man can change his skin to suit his background. And to function successfully, he has to as—with the exception of the arty element—the person who fails to blend in with his surroundings is always regarded with suspicion by the establishment.

This camouflage is best illustrated by the predominance of grey and blue as backdrop colours for city clothes and of green, khaki and brown in the country. It highlights the bold statement that a woman who adopts bright, striking colours in her dress is making.

A vibrant palette is considered perfectly acceptable by the seaside—on holiday, you are allowed to be daring and can wear bright, fun colours with impunity—but in more sober areas bright colours are sadly treated with caution.

Colour is a useful tool in the optical illusions department. By putting eye-catching colours (that is, bright or light) at the neck you are sure to divert attention to the face. And vice versa—wearing vivid shoes, stockings or gloves with a neutral outfit draws the observer's eye away from your face.

> Colour in dress is like tone of voice in speech in that it can completely alter the meaning of what is 'said' by other aspects of the costume: style, fabric and trimmings.

Alison Lurie
AUTHOR OF *THE LANGUAGE OF CLOTHES*

The juxtaposition of bright colours always produces exciting results but the proportions in which they're used can dramatically alter the effect. Play around until you find the happiest combination for you—not only your colouring but your mood too.

A suntan makes most people feel and look healthier. And once we have achieved a glowing tan, few of us pass up the chance to wear the strong, vivid shades that suit us temporarily. The skin tones of a bronzed body harmonize with orange and yellow and contrast stunningly with cobalt blue and fuchsia.

Bold colours are not only refreshing, but brave, especially when they are used for such a functional item as a winter coat. The blend of colours in this outfit (left) lives together in a marvellously unexpected but subtly harmonious mix, and goes to show that you can look vibrantly daring without striking a discordant note.

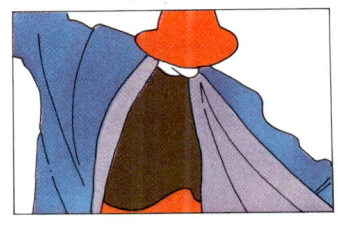

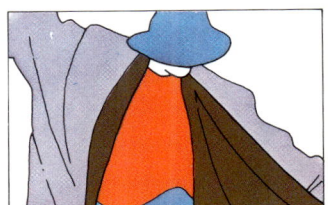 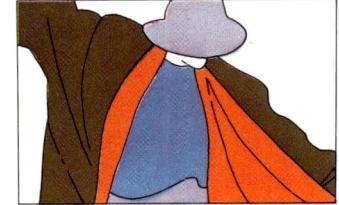

The emotions contained in this colour choice are a battleground. Red is the colour of love and anger and blue the shade of harmony, while black spells sophistication and lavender refinement. But however you combine the colours, the drama of the confrontation wins through.

109

Do you want the effect of your clothes to be feminine, pretty, sweet, cool, elegant and seductive? Then look no farther than the pastel spectrum. Luminous, translucent, always gentle, the appeal of pastels is that they have an almost subliminal effect. Instead of dominating your dress they allow you and your choice of shape and design a chance to star.

Pastel colours are created by adding white to the solid colours at the hub of the colour wheel. In theoretical terms they are called tints and in their pure form they all blend harmoniously. Traditionally pale colours are worn by the very young and the very old: sky blue, pink and lemon for babies and neutral shades for the elderly who for some sad reason often renounce colour as they get older.

Hence it is not surprising that until quite recently the image of pales and pastels was a bit saccharine – sugar pink, baby blue, peach. But with the successful introduction of greyed pales (some designers call them 'dirty'), pastel colours have achieved an elegant sophistication. Be careful when you mix these colours as greyed pastels can look discredited alongside a singingly clear tone. The same colour seen with companions of similar value, however – say misty taupe, cloudy violet and soft raspberry – can be heavenly.

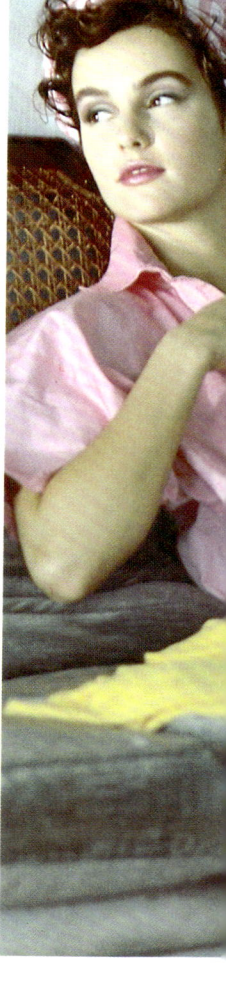

Bright pastels like hot pink and lemon retain the character of pastels in that they are emphatically feminine, but borrow the boldness and impact of primaries.

The palest pastels all blend harmoniously together – even if they are opposites on the colour wheel – as shown in these two beautiful tweed suits by Chanel.

CREAM TEASE

The neutral tones are not strictly pastels, but pale, non-colours. To wear these soft, sometimes drab, colours with success depends on your colouring. The cool glamour of this refined international taste suits many women including raven-haired and red-headed and has even earned a nickname when worn by blondes. But blonde on blonde, the stunning combination of blonde hair and clothes, rarely suits the naturally fair with an 'English Rose' complexion who tend to fade away under the beige tones. The natural blonde can wear beige with a suntan or together with a contrast colour, but she makes herself eminently missable if she wears it neat. It's a cruel irony that the success of the blonde on blonde formula is invariably the domain of the bottle- not the born- blonde.

Throughout the centuries, wearing all black or all white has been acknowledged as setting the wearer apart. Countless traditions—literary, religious, and secular—are all linked with dressing in these colours.

White stands for purity; it is the traditional colour in which to be christened, confirmed or, more recently, married. Today it may still spell innocence and simplicity but it is also, by virtue of its impracticality, the cheapest way to look expensive.

Black can be dramatic or sober, elaborate or expensive or merely hardwearing and economical because it doesn't show the dirt. But it is always sophisticated. Black is associated with grief, mourning and, in some countries, old age. Black is also the colour of rebellion. Teenagers from beatniks to punks have adopted it as a symbol of rejection of society's values.

Texture and pattern affect the colours we can wear. A colour combination that is normally hard can appear flattering when the fabric has a sheen, lustre or texture. Here black and white come up chequered in dogstooth and gingham and softened in silk, taffeta and wool.

BLACK AND WHITE DRAMA

If you are going all out for impact, no combination of colours will lend more dramatic weight than black and white. It is strident, jarring sometimes, but never insignificant. Many colour counsellors have suggested that this drama should be reserved for those of equally dramatic colouring. But this assumption, based on the success of harmonizing shades, ignores the stimulating effect of contrast.

Worn neat, black and white is chic, brash, but can be immensely harsh. Few people are advised to wear it unrelieved by other colours, jewellery or make-up.

Grey, the blend of black and white, is more conventional and self-effacing. Whether that describes the character of the 80's or not is open to discussion, but doyenne of the fashion world Diana Vreeland's prophetic statement 'Grey looks like being the beige of the 80's' has been emphatically borne out.

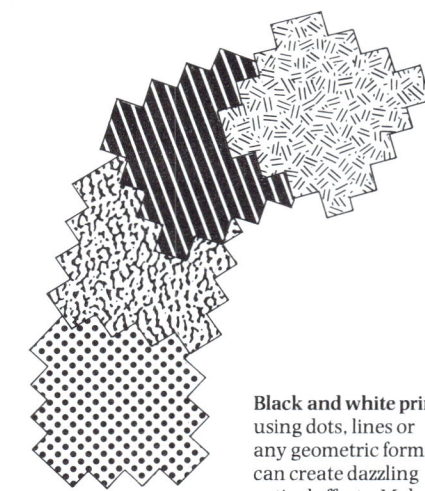

Black and white prints using dots, lines or any geometric forms can create dazzling optical effects. Make sure this dramatic impact works close up as well as at a distance.

THE VERSATILE WARDROBE

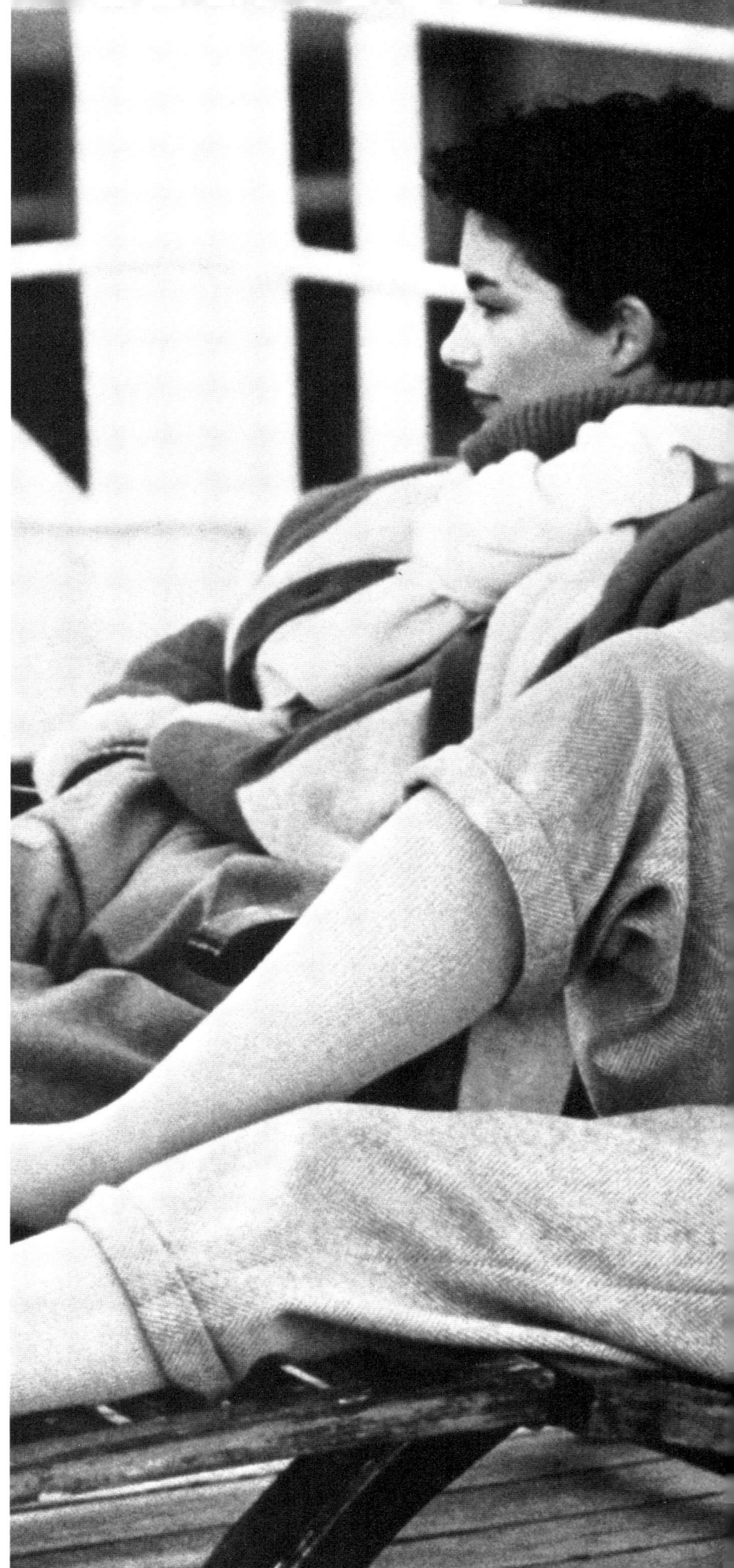

Versatile clothes are the ones that give you the most mileage. They can be contortionist clothes that delight in wrapping, rolling or folding themselves into countless different shapes to suit most aspects of your lifestyle. They can be clothes that you borrow and adapt or, quite simply, the items that have a knack of looking just about perfect for every occasion. Befriend them —they're your greatest ally.

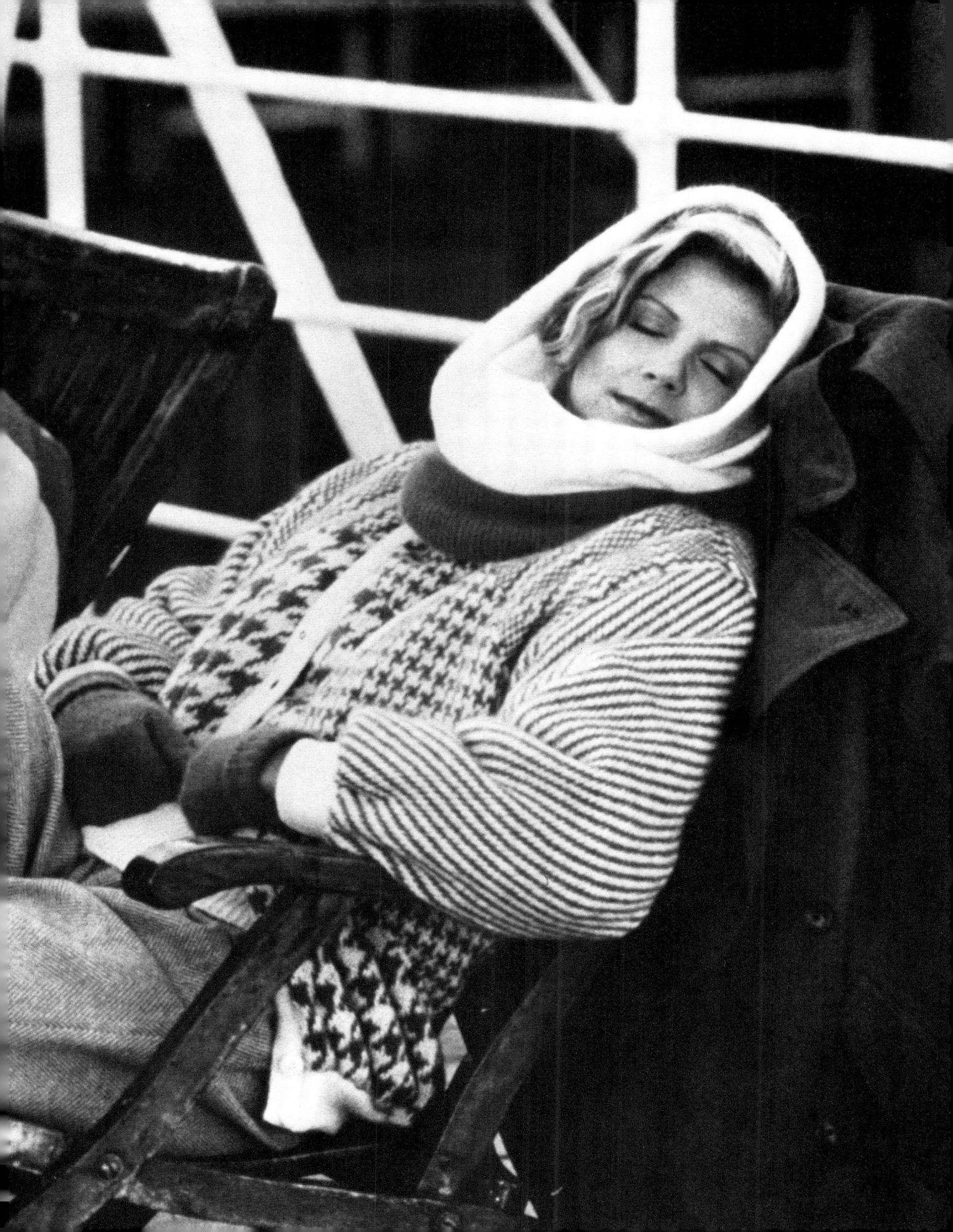

THE VERSATILE WARDROBE

First the bad news: there is no such thing as an all-purpose, go-anywhere outfit. A jogging suit that looks marvellous on the soccer terraces won't raise a ripple over drinks at the smartest club in town, and the suit that looks wonderful lunching in the city turns dreary and unappealing by the soft lights of a more homely setting. But the good news is that some garments have chameleon characters and can adopt a variety of guises to give them a number of different lives.

Take a sweater dress, for instance. The actual garment is adaptable enough to be worn – wrapped, tied or hitched up – in several different ways but its real bonus is that with an imaginative choice of accessories it will truly grace many occasions.

A sweater dress could be your most versatile buy, and, as it's sure to get lots of wear, there's one golden rule to help keep it in shape. When you sit down, hitch the dress up slightly so that while sitting you don't strain the stitches, and when you stand up the dress won't be seated.

All muffled up – just add thick tights, flat shoes and warm gloves and your sweater dress is fun for playdays.

116

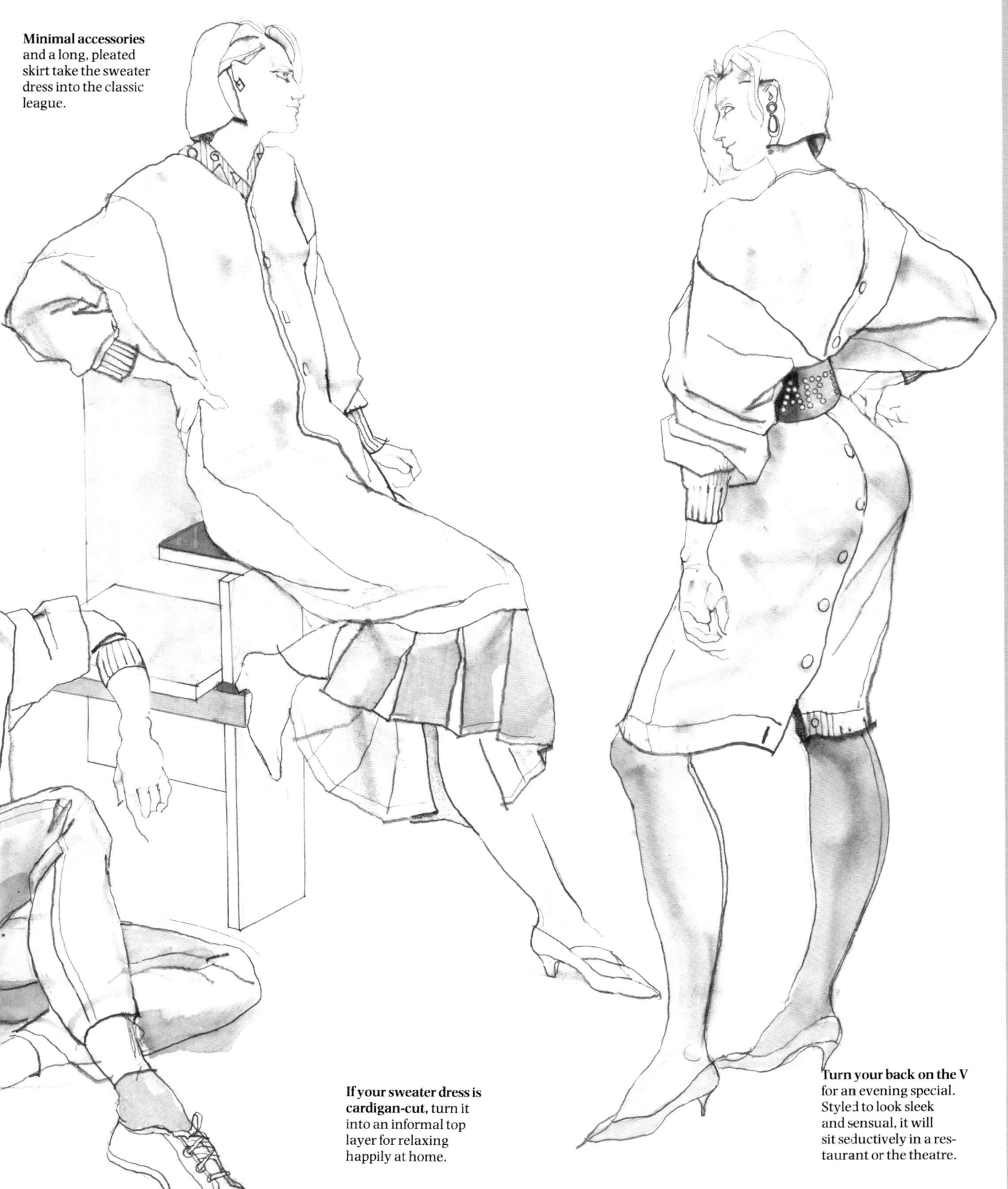

Minimal accessories and a long, pleated skirt take the sweater dress into the classic league.

If your sweater dress is cardigan-cut, turn it into an informal top layer for relaxing happily at home.

Turn your back on the V for an evening special. Styled to look sleek and sensual, it will sit seductively in a restaurant or the theatre.

117

Think of a dress that's comfortable and easy yet always manages to look smart and you're likely to be thinking of a shirtdress. All the permutations on the elongated-shirt theme – from casual shirtwaister to tuxedo-styled coatdress – share this easy quality.

The inherent character of the shirt- or coatdress is tailored and masculine, but the impression an individual style gives is determined more by its fabric and length than its design details. A full-length version, for instance, in slipper satin or matt jersey is the ideal choice for the sophisticated woman attending a gala occasion. In the same length, but switching the fabric to a cotton terry, the shirtdress becomes an elegant beach cover-up or lounging gown.

Shortening the skirt and opting for a stiff, candy-stripe cotton gives an efficient and crisp impression, whereas the same dress in linen will have a languid, leisurely air.

Turning up the hem once more, the dress becomes a big shirt. Wear it short and straight if your legs are great, hitched up with a hip-slung belt if they're sensational.

In its grown-up, elegant mood, the coatdress is well suited to simplicity (above) – accessorized with little more than a belt is often best.

But it is not averse to a more dressed-up approach (right) and can adapt itself to become a useful element in a heavily layered look.

FINISHING TOUCHES

The shirtdress has little hanger appeal, and it takes more than just a feminine body inside to give it impact. Whether it is buttoned up or open-necked alters the mood of a shirt- or coatdress to a degree, but it's the number of buttons you choose to leave undone at the hemline that really makes the difference.

Most shirtdresses come with their own self-fabric belts which are, of course, perfectly adequate. But for more polish substitute something in kid or suede. Belting in tightly is fine if your figure is well-proportioned, but if it tends towards the busty or hippy, a tight belt will only emphasize those areas. The hip-heavy girl often has an enviably tiny waistline, but in this instance she should resist the temptation to flaunt it.

THE ONE-OFF DRESS

The background basic is not the only dress to earn the 'versatile' tag. Surprisingly, any manner of fanciful concoction can fall into this category too – but for totally different reasons. The simple dress with its chameleon-like character is an obvious choice, but the highly fashionable and decoratively designed dress – which can be jolly pretty or jolly eccentric – can be equally successful.

If it's the dress you love to wear, and the one that suits you so well that you're happy to wear it almost anywhere – then it has to be good for your budget, however much it actually costs. You can wear it until it literally falls apart.

Treating the almost 'costume' – and usually expensive – dress as an essential part of a versatile wardrobe is a direct reversal of most people's ideas – it doesn't adapt, it doesn't change shape, and accessories rarely make an iota of difference to its strong statement. But as all its protagonists will tell you: 'Better to always look spectacular, even if that means wearing the same dress most of the time, than to play safe with endless permutations and always look merely acceptable.'

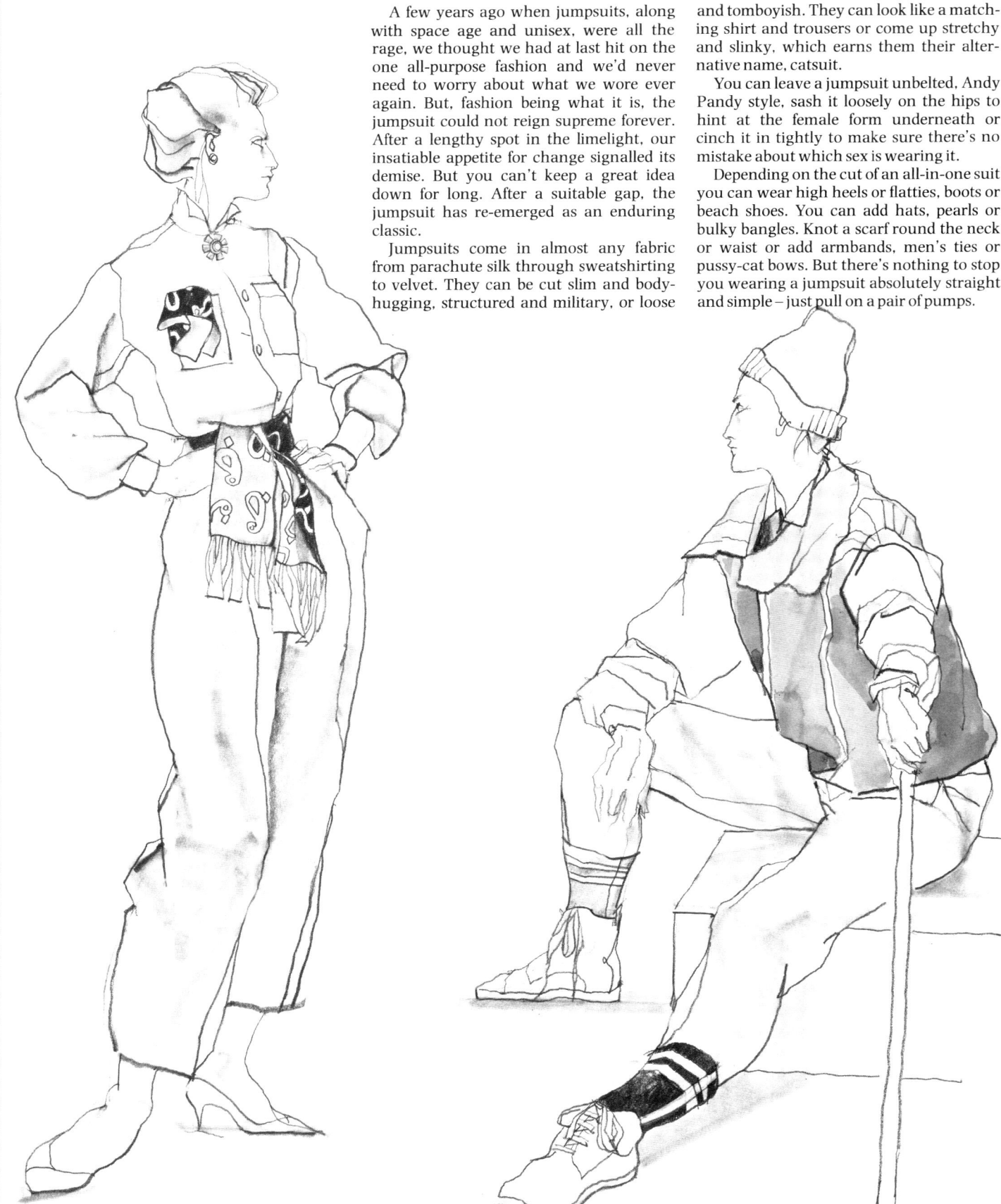

A few years ago when jumpsuits, along with space age and unisex, were all the rage, we thought we had at last hit on the one all-purpose fashion and we'd never need to worry about what we wore ever again. But, fashion being what it is, the jumpsuit could not reign supreme forever. After a lengthy spot in the limelight, our insatiable appetite for change signalled its demise. But you can't keep a great idea down for long. After a suitable gap, the jumpsuit has re-emerged as an enduring classic.

Jumpsuits come in almost any fabric from parachute silk through sweatshirting to velvet. They can be cut slim and body-hugging, structured and military, or loose and tomboyish. They can look like a matching shirt and trousers or come up stretchy and slinky, which earns them their alternative name, catsuit.

You can leave a jumpsuit unbelted, Andy Pandy style, sash it loosely on the hips to hint at the female form underneath or cinch it in tightly to make sure there's no mistake about which sex is wearing it.

Depending on the cut of an all-in-one suit you can wear high heels or flatties, boots or beach shoes. You can add hats, pearls or bulky bangles. Knot a scarf round the neck or waist or add armbands, men's ties or pussy-cat bows. But there's nothing to stop you wearing a jumpsuit absolutely straight and simple – just pull on a pair of pumps.

The real joy of the jumpsuit is its countless moods. Rolled up, casual and summery is how we know it best. But it is equally at home either plunged or buttoned up for chic evenings, or layered – both under and over – for colder climates.

There's something wonderfully jolly about wearing dungarees. Wear them roomy and baggy like a baby's rompers and you cast yourself in the role of an endearing, mischievous child. Dungarees are also a great equalizer: basically, everybody looks a bit shapeless in them – but who wants to play siren all the time?

For easy weekend wear they take some beating, and – worn the bigger the better – they will also hide a multitude of sins. They're great friends to girls whose bodies are on the large side but who, understandably, don't want to be condemned to tent dresses.

Unlike jumpsuits, dungarees don't really suit lots of fabrics. As they are truly utilitarian in shape, made up in anything other than workwear fabrics like drill, cord or denim they are either a sham or a short-lived gimmick.

You can buy dungarees from fashion shops, but some of the most successful and certainly the cheapest come from industrial uniform suppliers. Plumber's or carpenter's dungarees, for instance, come with all sorts of interesting pockets and zippered compartments to hold the tools of their trade. These details are your fashion touches.

Dungarees are seasonless and perfectly suited to layered dressing. As happy topping off a T-shirt as a thick rib sweater, they're equally content to partner fur-lined boots or strappy sandals.

You can wear them, body-flaunting, half undone over a chopped-up T-shirt – or even over nothing but a suntan. But for a more universal appeal, you'll find that when they're buttoned up they're great flaw-ignorers for less than perfect bodies.

121

We all play the game of fashion 'mathematics' with separates – add here, subtract there, and you've got a total look. But every so often when your arithmetic gets a bit rusty, it's a joy to rely on someone else's calculations.

Invest in a suit and you'll find that the sums are already done. When you want you can have a separates look, but you'll also always have that one special-occasion outfit in your wardrobe.

A coat is more formal than a jacket and a dress more so than separates, so a matching dress and coat is really only for very grand occasions. It's wonderful for winter weddings, especially if it's your turn to be mother of the bride.

It's very chic and relaxed to kit yourself out in figure-forming knits. But as most knitwear doesn't stay looking good forever, don't fall into the trap of over-ageing any one piece.

122

Borrowed from the boys is one thing, but adapted is another. A tuxedo suit is very definitely feminine once it is fitted and skirted.

Clever business-women always choose outfits like this that will divide up to live separate lives.

If you are dressing for success, a strictly tailored suit may work wonders – masculine white tie and all. But don't forget the feminine touches – white gloves, slim ankles in white hose and pretty pumps.

THE VERSATILE WARDROBE

Make your wardrobe a workshop of ideas. Time spent re-thinking, re-planning, adapting and fixing up new permutations and combinations will be time well invested. Never relegate clothes to a single area of your life. With a few exceptions like sundresses, duvet coats and taffeta gowns, almost all your clothes can be multipurpose.

Treat your clothes as seasonless items. Summer cottons, for instance, work just as well in cold climates. T-shirts can be worn as vests, summer jackets as winter shirts – or winter shirts as summer jackets. And white trousers worn over thermals make a lively contrast mid-winter.

Don't limit your clothes to their obvious moods. There is no rule to say that your dance leotard or swimsuit can't be worn as a classy evening top, that your winter thermals can't be put on show as summery vests and leggings, or that your structured, business blazer shouldn't shed its formal shirt and skirt, team up with a belt and a pair of trousers and go out to dinner all bare and beautiful.

When you borrow from his closet, don't forget to add or adapt. Flaunt a double cuff with *two* pairs of cufflinks, and strap too-long sleeves out of the way with a couple of belts.

On the subject of borrowing, the utility room need not be out of bounds. While all the fashion followers are sporting mock clothes pegs in their hair, show off your savvy with the real thing.

There's no reason why you shouldn't look absolutely ravishing on the beach wearing dad's old pyjamas. And while considering multi-use items, don't forget the ever-so-English sunhat trick with a knotted handkerchief. Update the idea by forsaking the hanky for a dishcloth – you'll find that it's far more glamorous.

124

BORROW FOR SUCCESS

James Bond's creator, Ian Fleming, is reputed to have said 'There's nothing sexier than a girl wearing a man's shirt.' And as most men happen to agree, this may explain why they don't mind so much when they find their best shirt is missing.

Over-sized men's shirts are the best steal we women ever made. Worn simply, they make striking mini shirtdresses or beach cover-ups, and matched up with trousers or a tailored skirt they become perfectly presentable for less casual wear. A big man's shirt is a great flatterer too, especially if you knot it blouson-style below the tummy.

Unusual or unexpected mixes are the spice that make fashion fun. Try out your own blend of contrariness. Why not mix a chunky-rib fisherman's sweater with a fancy, floral skirt? Or wear high-stepping pumps with your army fatigues, or even team up land-army breeches with a fragile blouse and lacy kerchief? And remember that sparkling junk gems give zest to all manner of workaday fabrics. It's the cunning contrast that demands attention.

The sailor's cap and the enormous chambray shirt worn here make passable partners, but what gives this outfit its edge is the almost over-abundance of diamanté jewellery.

125

Dressing in humble jumble, thrift shop buys and rummage-sale finds is synonymous with revamping old clothes. But don't forget that there are other options that are not always second-hand outlets. Men's outfitters, especially the cheap or the nearly-new variety, should appeal to the stylish bargain hunter. Men's clothes are usually of a better quality than women's and, with second-hand buys, there is less risk of the wear and tear showing through. But the main reason for cross-dressing is that girls look great in over-sized man's-styled shirts, suits, waistcoats and ties.

Catering and industrial clothes are another under-exploited source of cheap chic. Most of us know the possibilities of army surplus, but other uniforms are well worth investigating. Nurses' capes make dramatic cover-ups, gabardine school mackintoshes spell French style, Girl Guide outfits are crisp and clean-cut, and surely nobody needs reminding that painters' overalls are chic, cheeky and fun.

Some cheap or second-hand clothes need a little adapting – a tuck or a chop here and there help – but to make cheap clothes look cheerful, your biggest ally is a packet of dye. Plain fabrics like drill, cotton-knit and sweatshirting take best to a new coat of colour and the paler the shade of the original garment, the truer the end result. When choosing clothes to colour, remember – with dyeing you can only go darker.

Tie-dyeing is an effective variation. If you knot the fabric together or tie coins into the cloth with string, you'll make your own unique and individual pattern. Test out polyester or cotton dyes: if you use them on mixed-fibre fabrics, only bits will take and you'll achieve an interesting textured and tonal effect.

One of the best buys from a men's outfitters is a formal tailcoat. Nowadays it's almost as much of a fashion classic as the tuxedo and versatile enough to grace almost any evening occasion – as well as looking dandy by day teamed up with T-shirts, sweats and jeans.

The chef's elegant, side-buttoning jacket is a faultless piece of design which is far too good to be left in the kitchen. Wear it open and relaxed or buttoned up and belted. And his gingham trousers which come checked, cropped and casual, need only to be cinched in at the waist for instant appeal.

126

Wearing vintage clothes ensures a certain eccentricity and certainly saves you from the clone-like quality that chain-store clothes can bestow.

You can wear your period pieces in their natural context and achieve a nostalgic, almost fancy-dress style or contemporize them with brand new accessories to look as fresh and bright as paint.

A feeling for nostalgia makes for more second-hand-roses than a tiny budget. And marvellous old and antique clothes can still be found. Listed here are a few of the best sources, including the nearly-new for more recent cast-offs.

Jumble sales are good for men's clothes, outgrown, but not worn-out, knitwear, and the occasional inspired find like a model dress or 1930's teagown. You can tell an area by its jumble, so if you're in this market, check the local press for details of sales in the more wealthy districts. Get there early, before the dealers have snapped up all the interesting buys. There is no control on the condition of the clothes, but with prices from a few pence to rarely more than a pound for anything, this should not matter.

Dress agencies are another word for nearly-new shops. It is difficult to categorize their stock as it consists of other people's mistakes, or items they have grown tired of. It is sometimes totally up-to-the-minute, but usually a season or two behind the current trends. These sources are great for classics, but buy fad items with care. Clothes should be clean and as good as new – expect to pay about a third or less of their original shop price.

Charity or thrift shops sell better-condition jumble. Everything will be clean, but not necessarily mended. What you find depends on the generosity and style of the people in the area – and their knowledge (if they don't realize that an old beaded gown is worth a fortune at auction they may pack it off to the thrift shop). The local old-age pensioners and school children often contribute by producing hand-knits and craft items that can be well-made and lovely. Prices are rising steadily to match the demand and what people are prepared to pay, but it is still possible to pick up a good party frock for under ten pounds. If you don't mind stepping into dead men's shoes, charity shops are also good for vintage footwear.

A mix of white cotton and lace is quite the freshest thing you can wear – and what's more its softness, crispness and feminine styling suits almost everyone regardless of shape or size. It does demand looking after though.

Antique shops are a reliable if costly hunting ground for lace accessories. And a little bit of lace works wonders when it comes to dressing up your clothes. A lace collar or jabot (top) will pretty up the coolest of dresses.

This outfit would cost a fortune if you bought it from a classy boutique, but it could just as easily have been put together from a stack of bargain finds. You'll find lacy shawls at thrift shops or church hall fêtes, and second-hand Fairisle knits going for a song at the neighbourhood jumble sale.

Lace can be as daring as it is demure and the very brave can be immodest with a 'modesty' (left). The lacy bodice is what the Victorians wore as an undergarment to preserve their modesty but it makes a stunning if flamboyant evening top. And worn with expressive silks or suede it adds a bohemian touch of spirit.

Second-hand stores have clothes bought in bulk from local authorities, house sales and wholesale clearances. There is a cross-Atlantic travel in used clothes. The Americans send the British baseball jackets, Hawaiian shirts, tuxedos, military kit and wool overcoats and the British send second-hand, but more period pieces like lace blouses, bespoke shirts and waiter's wear to the States. Prices in Britain are usually rock bottom; in the States they can be quite high, but the quality is often quite high too.

Antique shops and auctions specialize in the type of clothes that we all wish our ancestors had stored for us, but didn't. With popular items like Victorian nightdresses, the clothes can cost as much or more than their modern equivalents, but if you develop a taste for the exotic rather than the popular you will make far keener bargains. Look out for evening coats or anything with an oriental flavour.

With antique clothes the quality and the workmanship are usually superb but, unless you are an expert seamstress, don't buy anything that needs altering too drastically. Modern dry cleaning methods spell death to ancient, delicate fabrics so, unless you have the confidence to hand-wash or dye, avoid anything that is badly stained.

129

First forget the old theory that prints should only be worn with plains. As long as there is a colour connection you can mix prints with abandon. If you're mixing in major doses, it's wise to stick with small patterns such as floral sprigs and paisley designs or the once-ungodly combination of stripes, spots and checks. But there's nothing to stop a mix of cabbage roses and abstract splashes looking spectacular – in fact some of the world's greatest designers, notably Kenzo and Ungaro, have made their names doing just that.

In the hands of the experts, mixing patterns is an art form. When you are improvising at home, take things gently at first to build up your confidence and your eye for colour. You'll find that combining patterns in different weights of fabric often gives the best results, as in the photograph below. Don't forget the attraction of opposites in a mix like soft stripes and Fairisles.

Prints can also be used as a form of camouflage. Just as the wavy lines of military camouflage break up the exact outlines of a plane or tank, so too can patterned fabrics in dress. But if the disguise of, say, too much bulk is your aim, don't let the pattern be too eye-catching or it will defeat the object.

Some prints simply must stand on their own. Either their statement is too bold to be diluted by other designs, or their impact is so strong that it would jumble in the company of others. Take jungle prints or figurative designs, both of which make other patterns superfluous. Striking prints are often best cut into simple shapes to give the pattern an uninterrupted stage. A straight shift works well but, better still, find a richly patterned scarf or shawl that will add zest to almost everything you own.

This girl could hardly have combined more patterns and textures in one outfit, but it works spectacularly. Although every item she is wearing contrasts in weave, fibre, fabric or material, each one picks up on a colour link, however tenuous.

This type of pattern mixing takes skill, confidence and a sure eye. See how the aqua of the ribbed wool sleeves and the deep sea green of the leather jacket are mirrored in the curly astrakhan of the fez, picked up in the jacquard pattern of the gloves and hinted at in the silver of the bangles, ring and earrings.

The jewellery is the clue to the colour thread. The amber of the earrings is repeated in the orange of the paisley tie and in the hectically printed shirt which leads to the chrome of the diamond print scarf.

Liberty of London is famous throughout the world for superior design and excellent fabrics. Liberty has always been a forerunner and exponent of major trends: Art Nouveau, for instance, is even known as *Stile Liberty* in Italy.

The 'Liberty bank' of fabrics is huge. There are always 16 of the classic prints available and new ones are introduced every season. Some of the 'new' designs are brand new, others achieve the same freshness by reworking earlier prints in new fabrics or colours.

❝ To create a contemporary feel for the 80's (right), we decided on a mix of checks, tartans, plains and the more traditional but ever-popular floral prints. ❞

John Leflin
DESIGN DIRECTOR, LIBERTY

An outfit in one texture, like one in a single colour, can be spectacular if you have the grooming to carry it off. But like tones in colour, adventure with texture is what gives our clothes variety and appeal. A mix of weights in one outfit such as silk organza, damask and crepe de Chine or wool jersey, challis and worsted not only provide added interest, but give an adaptable separates feel and a combination of coolness and cover.

Some cloths have inherent qualities peculiar to them. Think of the tactile fabrics like velvet, chenille and suede or the crispness one associates with certain types of cotton like piqué and poplin, the strength and durability of denim or the drape of matt jersey.

The choice of fabric for a basic garment like a simple shirt can totally change its character. A silk shirt denotes dressing up, for instance, and linen will always spell sophistication. Cotton rarely rises above workaday and a cotton and wool mix like Viyella will always be cosy.

The way a particular fabric falls has a tremendous influence on the final appearance of a garment. If you look at a sketch of a dress on the drawing board without knowing what fabric it will be made up in, you can have no idea how the end result will look. Whatever the cut, some fabrics like cotton jersey or satin hug or cling to the body whereas others like calico and tweed stand away from it.

Juxtaposing fabrics is a stimulating approach to design. A beret made in satin, for instance, or a taffeta trenchcoat or a denim bikini makes its impact with the surprise element of the fabric.

With classic clothes there can be nothing unexpected. When we refer to classic tailored trousers, it is understood that they are made in something equally classic such as drill or flannel, and a V neck sweater is only a classic if it is knitted in a traditional yarn like cashmere or lambswool. Knit it in mohair and it enters a different category altogether.

One of the most important things about texture is the part it plays in selling clothes, as cloth is often the vital factor. When a woman looks at a rail of clothes she cannot see the style of a garment, nor can she read the price – but she is drawn to the fabric.

In fashion opposites always attract. Think of the lure of leather and lace or the appeal of country tweed teamed with sophisticated velvet. And when mohair meets chiffon sparks fly. Mohair is probably the softest wool and chiffon the softest silk, but there the similarity ends. One is bulky and opaque, the other fine and sheer. One feels warm and wrapped up, the other by contrast appears cool and bared, but mix them together for a sensation. It's not necessarily a classic or may not even be to your taste, but that's the joy of frivolous fashion – it's all down to personal fancy and individual choice.

Suede, soft as butter, and leather, supple as silk have brought about a whole new way of wearing skin (right). No longer reserved for hard, masculine shapes, leather is now fluid enough to knot nonchalantly and suede can be supple enough to be shirred into an elasticated waist. This is leather and suede at its most relaxed and luxurious.

JAPANESE TEXTURES

Elaborate texture blending is the hub of the recent Japanese design success. The simple (though intricately cut) shapes make their impact with richly textured contrasts.

Issey Miyake, who is probably the most inventive of the Japanese design contingent, uses the fabric as the starting point for all his designs. His shapes are always dictated by the quality of the fabric. He does not cut and sew, but creates his own unique lines by using the body as a frame over which he drapes shapes which move naturally with the body. This Miyake outfit demonstrates the wealth of weights, textures and weaves that under his skilful hand are so adeptly worked together.

> ❝ Borrowing the easy and adaptable attributes of the kimono makes it possible to appreciate the beauty of both the fabric and of the human body and, in addition, the harmony that can be created when both are allowed expression. ❞

Issey Miyake
FASHION DESIGNER

THE NATURAL FACTOR

Natural fibres like wool, silk, cotton and linen wear well and feel good to wear, but they are more expensive than their man-made counterparts and demand more rigorous care and upkeep. Recent developments mean that some synthetic fabrics are verging on the excellent – inexpensive, enduring and attractive to the touch as well as being in many cases wash-and-wear. But they still have a serious and, to many people, insurmountable drawback. The scientists have yet to develop a fibre that allows the body to breathe easily, so all man-made fabrics have a tendency to make you perspire. If you are not a confirmed natural-fibre fanatic, why not try a fabric with a high proportion of natural to synthetic fibres? It may offer the best of both worlds.

ACCESSORIES

'It's not what you wear, it's the way that you wear it', is only half the story. What you wear *with* 'it' is what gives you and your personality a real chance to come into the equation. It may be a cliché, but it's the truth — a change of accessories can totally alter the character of an outfit.

THE REAL THING

Think real and you automatically think classy – and expensive. But, be it a bag, a belt or a bangle, 'expensive' need not mean 'ludicrous'. A slim gold chain, for instance, need not cost more than an extravagant piece of paste, for the gold is real, dateless and always looks great.

Real pieces are investments – a Rolex watch, the classic Hermès 'Kelly' bag, a perfect string of pearls – and since you will probably want to wear them with everything, they could just work out as bargains when it comes to cost per wear. Be sure you truly love items at these price levels; and don't be seduced by designer labels for their own sake. Identify the quality as well, recalling the slogan Botega Veneta use to promote their leather goods . . . 'When your own initials are enough'.

If you are diffident about joining this league, you can still be 'real', with natural wooden beads rather than copy-cat gems.

DAZZLING DIANA

In the recession-hit 70's it seemed rather tacky to flaunt any wealth that was left, but now that the world looks as though it can see the end of the tunnel, looking expensive and well-turned out is once again acceptable. Two of the greatest protagonists of the return to style (with a capital E for expensive) are Princess Diana and Nancy Reagan. Neither are afraid to wear real – in clothes, accessories and most importantly in jewels.

The Princess's taste in jewellery, along with her taste in clothes, has changed considerably with her new role. As a young girl she wore the fripperies of the debutantes' set – a gold D on a slim chain, a man's chunky watch and gold hoop earrings. Nowadays she has one of the largest and most valuable jewellery collections in the world at her disposal. The cream of her collection consists of family heirlooms from both the Spencer and, of course, the Windsor side, as well as the almost priceless presents given to her by the world's heads of state on her wedding day.

Here the Princess of Wales is shown wearing a glittering, sunray diamond necklace, a piece that she often borrows from the Queen. It has a dual role in that, with the addition of a frame, it can be worn as a tiara. Her diamond and pearl earrings were just one part of the generous wedding gift from the Crown Prince of Saudi Arabia.

ACCESSORIES

Anything goes when you're young and fashion is purely for fun. But if you follow the latest gimmick, fad or whimsy, you've boarded the fashion merry-go-round, and once on, you have to keep at it – there's nothing so dated as last week's look. With small, disposable accessories like hair pegs or cheap synthetic scarves the cost may not matter, and when it comes to the more costly items, high fashion's built-in obsolescence isn't as unkind as most people think. Hang on to anything that is good but momentarily past its peak, and it will probably return as a fashion classic within a few seasons.

The way you wear accessories can change the tempo of your clothes. Take belts: slung across your hips a belt makes an entirely different statement from one that is tightly buckled up, and it also does totally different things for your figure. If you are not as slim as you'd like, never belt up too tightly and avoid wide belts that might accentuate your bulges. Choose extravagant buckles that divert attention or opt for supple sashes that soften the silhouette.

It's a wrap – get knotted and be your own hair 'dresser'. Take lengths of fabric, scarves or scraps of lace and wrap, tie, knot and clip your way to a piccaninny-style head.

A simpler way to tie yourself in knots is to opt for the turban. Sleek, dramatic and the best solution for hair that needs a cut or a wash. The frothy bandeau looks cute, especially if it is framed with curls, and a bandanna tied straight around the head is riveting in light colours as it highlights the eyes.

Dressing your hair need not stop at scarves or conventional combs and clips. Colourful pegs grip the hair with a vengeance so you don't have to worry about them slipping, and rubber styling shapers make for an amusing twist.

Jokey accessories can liven up a trad outfit. A pair of day-glo specs looks unexpected and sensational with sober suiting, and daft earclips add humour to almost anything. But if you want the joke to be truly on you, the silly bits must match the mood of the clothes you're wearing.

139

ACCESSORIES

Fashion has a lot to do with breaking rules and when it comes to dressing up our clothes, there are more rules to break than ever. Those that guided our mothers have little relevance today. They were told that once they were dressed they should look in a mirror and remove one item. For them the rule was better to be under-dressed than over-accessorized. For today's minimalist looks, where accessorizing with more than a watch is considered over the top, our mother's maxim is nearly right. But when it comes to the glitzy side of the business, the more the merrier generally is the rule.

Flashy and fake doesn't have to mean junk. Frankly fake accessories are the ones that don't pretend to be anything else. It's not a case of rubber masquerading as leather or glass as diamonds, but rubber or paste as bold, brash fashion items in their own right.

Fake items tend to be the bigger ones in your accessory collection, which makes them the ones to use in order to accentuate your best features. So if you've got a great waistline – belt it; if you have striking eyes – let earrings draw attention to them; with pretty hands – use a bold cuff or distinctive watch to get them noticed. But their very boldness also makes them the most likely contenders for mistakes. Never wear a choker round a plump or short neck, wide rings on short, stubby fingers or a large bag if you are very small – it will appear to be carrying you. Don't hang a shoulder bag on a heavy area like hips. Adjust the strap so that the bag hangs at the top of your hipbone.

SPECS BEFORE YOUR EYES

The one accessory you wear on your face can't be hidden, however pale the frames. Choose shapes that suit (like rounded frames for a square face) whether your lenses are optical or for sun-screening. If you are short-sighted, your lenses will make your eyes and face outline appear smaller; go for small frames and tint across the lens to minimize distortion. Lenses for long sight magnify eyes; too large a frame will make you goggle-eyed. Perfect a flawless eye make-up as any mistakes will be dramatically on show.

Spots and stripes may mean camouflage in the jungle, but worn on a city street they shriek of exhibitionism, especially when worn neat. Edit the skin-stealing down to, say, a fur hat, belt or gloves for a more elegant fakery.

Coco Chanel invented costume jewellery. She was the first to suggest that junk gems could be as stylish as the real thing. Ropes of baroque pearls, strings of glass and gilt, huge pearl and gilt earclips and paste pieces as dramatic as the Ritz are now the signature of the House of Chanel. 'Pile it on' is the philosophy and, coupled with the under-statement of the clothes, these fabulous pieces never even hint at the vulgar.

ACCESSORIES

Native, tribal, indigenous: ethnic encompasses a multitude of exotica, the best of which is natural, original and breathtakingly beautiful, the worst nasty and mass-produced, to be avoided at all costs. Good ethnic can be as much of an investment as serious gemstones. When you buy Navaho beads or Caribbean coral you are purchasing thousands of years of heritage as well as something pretty to wear round your neck.

Think of ethnic accessories and everyone will envisage something different. It could be a Chinese chopstick for your hair, a Ralph Lauren silver and turquoise conch belt or any number of treasures found in the Indian, African or Russian continents. But ethnic doesn't have to come from far-away places. Designers take their inspiration from as many varied sources as possible and as long as any interpretation is handled with talent it is not only valid but worthy in its own right.

Unless you are using ethnic in a fancy dress fashion, try to limit your pieces. One stunning armlet or necklace will have a much stronger impact than an over-kill by the addition of rings, earrings and belt too.

If you are searching for truly unique looks, ethnic is your easiest avenue. Anyone with half an eye for colour or combination can string together an arbitrary but stunning selection of seashells, glass beads, pebbles and wood chips.

Accessories can totally change the character of your clothes. The truth of this particular fashion cliché is dramatically demonstrated in Avedon's photograph for Alexon. Top model Iman is wearing an outfit by Alexon, who make sound, classic clothes with a strong, contemporary fashion edge. But what a difference a few, or rather a lot of, beads and bangles make.

143

There's absolutely nothing new about girls wearing boys' clothes. Every generation of women this century – and some from the last – seem to have shared a fascination with their menfolk's cupboards or tailors at some stage in their lives. Each time a fresh foray is made, the effect is just that little bit different. And the 'difference' is almost always down to accessories.

The recent 'street credible' trend for androgynous style relies heavily on traditional menswear for its gender-bending impact but achieves its originality mostly for its lack rather than its display of accessories. Starkly simple is the 80s' route to suitability.

Wearing menswear is not meant to be fancy dress; rather, it's a chic and uncomplicated way of daytime dressing. When women adopt the look and acquire a man-sized suit and overcoat it's only a short step to purchasing Jermyn Street shirts and a few of his accoutrements too.

A tie (preferably club stripe, spotted or plain), a positive, masculine watch and an exquisite pair of cufflinks are the most that's called for. If your fancy runs to other areas of his wardrobe, exercise control. Armbands, silk evening scarves, mufflers, briefcases, bow ties and even medals are all perfectly permissible, as long as they are worn in strict moderation.

'The dandy' is quite a different matter. Firstly, it's a period style that looks best by night in all its decorative glory and anyway would be far too ornate to fit into most women's daytime styles. And secondly, unless your man happens to be extremely foppish or an ardent fan of Oscar Wilde, the clothes won't be readily available for you to raid.

The accessories needed to complete the look – fob watches, Albert chains, brocade waistcoats, spats, canes, button boots and wing collars – will have to be special purchases too, or at a pinch a family heirloom or even a gift from a generous great-grandfather.

Brace yourself and belt up if you want to wear the widest parallel pants. The strength of this look is its simplicity and its androgynous quality – without the turban it would look as good on him as her.

RIGHT ON TIME

If you own several watches, among them will be a sports or all-round watch – either a chuck-away fun piece like a rubber-cased disposable or a *grande marque* such as a Rolex Oyster or Cartier Santos, or one of the rubber-strapped Ferrari or Hublot models – or something cheaper along the same lines. The ideal watch wardrobe also includes a dress watch, preferably a vintage version. The joy of an antique watch is that it takes you out of the status rat race that surrounds all the new models.

Every now and again a fad watch catches the collective imagination, witness the success of childish Mickey Mouse clock-watches or the cute little robot watches. They make great conversation pieces for now and possibly collectors items later.

Dress up like a dandy with not one but three fob watches. But remember that it could be time for the chop. However fancy this look may be, it is definitely not a feminine one. So if you don't want to lop off your locks, tuck them up and out of the way in a dignified knot.

If you're often guilty of saying 'I haven't anything to wear' when looking at a wardrobe full of clothes, think hard about the possible reasons for this. If you look after your clothes well, you will always have something suitable ready to wear.

However much of a hurry you're in, always hang clothes up while they're still warm from the heat of your body, so that the creases have a chance to drop out. But don't put them in a wardrobe straight away – allow time for the air to circulate round them first. Close zips and buttons to help a garment keep its shape.

Invest in a really good stiff clothes brush and give your clothes a thorough brushing before you put them away to remove hairs, dandruff and surface dirt and dust. Use sticky tape wound round your hand, sticky side out, to get rid of hairs and stubborn pieces of fluff. It's not a good idea to wear any garment two days running – clothes last longer and look fresher if they recover before being worn again.

If your clothes get soaked or muddy, hang them up where they can dry naturally – don't drape them over a radiator or near an open fire. When the garment's completely dry, remove the hard mud with a stiff brush, then wash or dry clean it if necessary. Remove rain marks from leather by wiping it with a clean damp cloth, and from suede by brushing it. If fur gets wet, hang it in a cool place with air circulating round it – not in a cupboard. Never brush or comb furs, just shake them out. Regular cleaning by a specialist is important.

Never put dirty clothes away – drop them straight into a washing basket, or put them to one side for dry cleaning. In fact, don't ever wait until your clothes are really dirty before washing or cleaning them – it makes it harder to restore them to their original condition. Deal with any stains as soon as they appear (see pages 150–151); if left, they attract moths and mildew, as well as being more difficult to remove.

A STITCH IN TIME

Do any small repairs to your clothes before they become big ones – or, if you *know* you're never going to get round to it, or if you don't want to risk spoiling a special item, use the dry cleaner's repair service.

Keep an emergency sewing kit to hand – it will encourage you to keep your clothes in good repair. It should contain: a packet of assorted needles; a box of sharp dressmaking pins (throw out any rusty ones); a thimble; a pair of small scissors; a seam ripper; a tape measure; several reels of cotton, including black, white and some strong button thread – if you very rarely sew, buy a multicoloured plait instead.

It's also worth keeping a stockpile of zips and an assortment of buttons, as well as hooks and press studs. Thread matching buttons on a length of thread. Include some iron-on mending tape too.

SHOE CARE

It's often said that you can tell a person's character by the state of their shoes, which may prompt you to take care of your own.

To preserve their shape, always use a shoe horn when you put them on and put shoe trees inside when you take them off. Polish leather shoes frequently. You can buy a shoe cream to protect shoes against wet – it's worth applying this to brand new shoes, especially light coloured ones. Leather is likely to dry and crack with age, but leather oil or saddle soap helps to keep it supple.

If your shoes do get badly marked or scuffed, look for a renovating polish in a toning shade. Have soles and heels mended as soon as they need it – and well before they wear right through.

Wet shoes can be damaged by heat, so don't leave them by a radiator or an open fire. Dry them slowly in a warm room, but away from direct heat; pack the insides with crumpled newspaper, replacing it when it becomes damp.

● Store black clothes inside out, to prevent them picking up dust and fluff.

● To hang up a long evening dress without the hem touching the floor, sew loops on the inside at waist level. Turn the dress inside out and hang it like a skirt.

● Turn glittery metallic evening clothes inside out to prevent them catching on other garments.

● Tops made of synthetic fabric are better rolled than folded before being put away.

● Line the drawer in which you keep tights and stockings with self-adhesive plastic to stop them snagging on splinters in the wood.

● To stop small hooks making a bulge in the back of jackets or dressing gowns, spear a small, sponge-rubber ball on each hook – or sew a hanging loop to the inside of your clothes.

● Never leave a silk garment in direct sunlight or the colours will fade.

● After a swim, don't just hang your swimsuit up to dry, but rinse it in tap water first. The salt in seawater and the chemicals in swimming pools can eventually damage the material.

● Always hang wet or damp clothes on plastic hangers – wood or metal can stain them.

● Wear a scarf with a suede or leather coat to prevent grease marks round the neck.

● Give suede and sheepskin coats a stiff brushing when you take them off.

● If you have a suede suit, always take both pieces to be cleaned together, otherwise there could be a slight colour variation.

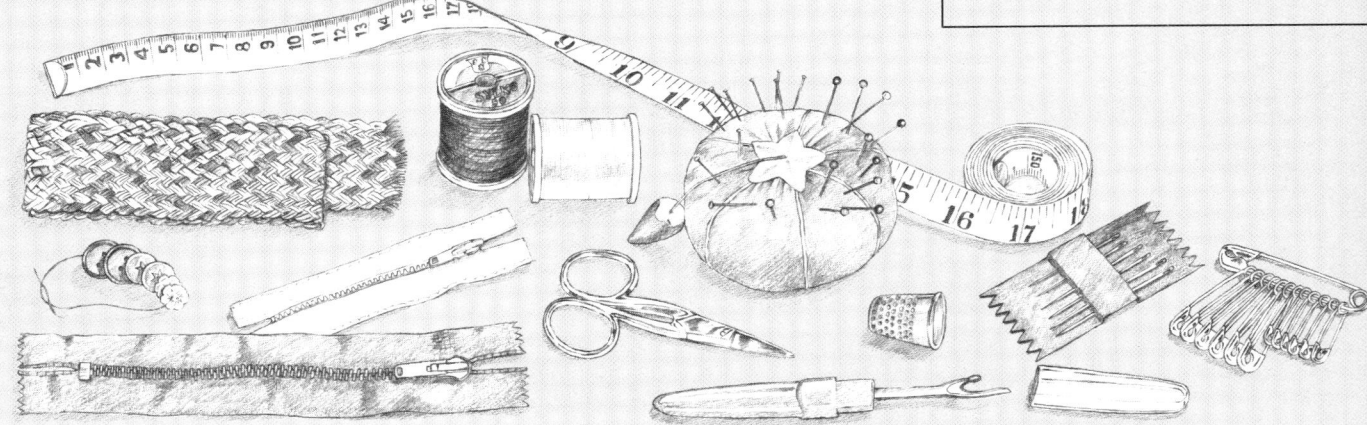

STORING CLOTHES

Very few of us ever feel we have enough space to store our clothes – but are you making the best use of the space you have? The illustration for Planning a Wardrobe on pages 20-21 suggests an ideal way to store all manner of garments, but your own storage may dictate a different solution.

Make the most of limited wardrobe space by hanging all your clothes facing the same way. Leave as much space between hangers as you can, to stop your clothes creasing too much and to allow air to circulate around them.

If you have a tie rack on the inside of your wardrobe, use it for scarves. Hang belts up in the wardrobe too if you can (eg. on hooks inside the wardrobe door) – it not only helps to keep your wardrobe neat and clear, but if scarves and belts catch your eye as you're getting dressed you're likely to get more wear out of them. Large scarves and shawls can be folded and kept with your knitwear.

Sweaters, knitted dresses and shirts can be folded and stored flat, in a drawer or on a shelf within the wardrobe. Keep gloves together in an old shoe box, near your coat.

If you're short of hanging space, pack away out-of-season clothes. Make sure each item is clean and check it over for missing buttons, fallen hems or broken zips. Fold each item separately, preferably interleaving with tissue paper to minimize creasing. Store them individually in polythene bags, or in a plastic packaway wardrobe or even in a suitcase. Make sure they're in a well-ventilated room to stop them being attacked by moths or damp.

If you own a fur coat, take special care that it's properly stored. Keep it in a cotton or silk bag and hang it on a padded hanger with plenty of space around it.

FOLDING A SHIRT

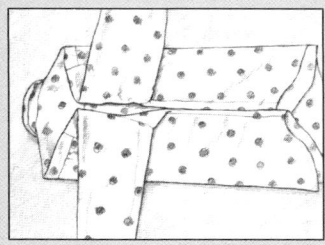 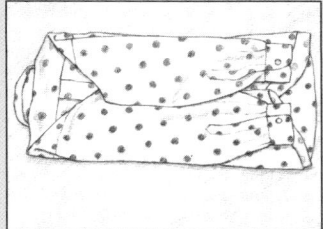 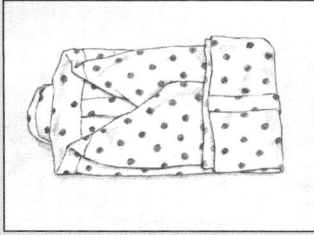 

1 Place the buttoned-up shirt face down on a table. Fold the side seams to the centre back.

2 Lay the sleeves flat along the folded edge, with the underarm seams in the centre.

3 Turn the bottom of the shirt up about a third, together with the sleeve cuffs.

4 Fold again, about halfway up. Sweaters and jackets should be folded in a similar way.

PREPARING TO PACK

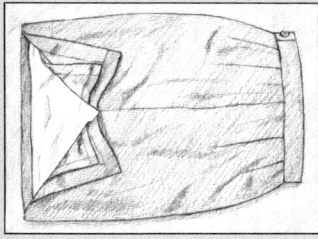 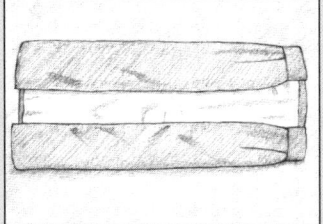 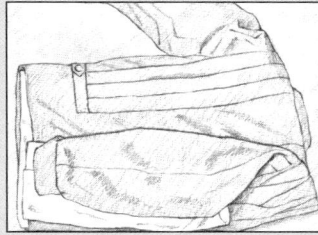 

1 Put a sheet of tissue paper between a skirt and its lining.

2 With the skirt flat, lay tissue down the middle before folding the side seams towards the centre.

1 Put tissue paper inside the sleeves of a jacket, as well as using it at every folding stage.

2 A ball of tissue stops a jacket being flattened. Socks fill gaps along case sides and reduce movement.

PACKING A SUITCASE

Whether you're packing for a holiday or a sales conference, you want your clothes to remain as crease-free as possible. The key to this is to use lots of tissue paper, laying it inside each garment at every folding stage as well as putting it between layers of clothing in the suitcase. Make sure you always put the heaviest clothes at the bottom.

To make the most of the space, stuff shoes with socks or panties, lay belts flat, not rolled, and decant your shampoo and beauty products into smaller plastic bottles.

You can buy inflatable hangers if you need to take your own.

If you travel a lot you'll find a travel iron useful – they can be surprisingly light and they pack away to take up very little room in a suitcase, as the handle folds down.

● Fold trouser legs along the creases, with the side seams together. Put tissue inside each leg and between the legs.

● Turn culottes the same way as trousers but then treat them as a skirt.

● Hang your clothes up as soon as you arrive, and light creases should drop out. More stubborn ones can usually be steamed out by hanging clothes over a bath full of hot water or somewhere they won't get wet while you are showering.

CARE AND REPAIR

It's very easy to just throw all your clothes into an automatic washing machine, select an average programme and hope for the best. But items may shrink, colours may run and some clothes will not be clean.

Care labels attached to your clothes will tell you how each item is to be washed and dried. If there is no care label, it is required by law that manufacturers identify the fibre content of a garment, from which you can work out how best to treat your clothes.

Most fabrics, especially synthetics, should be washed frequently to keep them looking their best. Once dirt has become ingrained or stains allowed to set, it may be too late to ever get your clothes really clean again. A fluorescent agent is often added to white fabrics which gradually breaks down with wear, so frequent washing is necessary to preserve the whiteness for as long as possible. Most launderettes have a maximum temperature of 60°C. At this temperature, the bleaching agent in the washing powder will not be sufficiently activated to get white clothes really white. As long as you're only washing whites, you could add bleach to your wash to counteract this.

Always be sure to rinse your clothes well. Cleaning agents left in fabric can irritate the skin and permanently damage clothes.

The basic washing symbol; the number indicates the full washing process.

Chlorine (household) bleach may be used.

Do not machine wash. Hand washing instructions may be added in another box.

Do not use chlorine bleach.

The number in the tub indicates the maximum water temperature.

Article may be tumble dried.

Article must not be washed at all.

Do not tumble dry.

This is the basic drying symbol.

Dry flat.

May be dried on a line.

Drip-dry.

Do not dry clean.

Garment may be dry cleaned in all solvents.

Underlining indicates that professional procedures are required.

Garment may be dry cleaned in perchlorethylene, white spirit, or solvents 11 and 113.

HAND WASHING
Sophisticated though most washing machines are these days, it may still be advisable to hand wash more delicate items, especially silks and woollens, or fabrics with special finishes. Non-fast coloureds that shed their dyes readily should be washed by hand so that they are immersed in water for no longer than necessary.

Cotton and linen Wash in water as hot as you can stand (wear rubber gloves). Make a good lather and rub, knead or scrub with a soft brush. Rinse and wring thoroughly. Whites can be boiled if heavily soiled, but linens may shrink. Colourfast cottons and linens can be washed in the same way, but do not boil. Try to avoid rubbing printed items as the colours may run.

Drip-dry cottons These should be washed frequently as the resin used to produce the special finish tends to attract dirt that can be hard to remove once it has become ingrained. Wash them by hand in plenty of hot water and suds, using a soft brush to loosen the dirt, as this creases less than rubbing. Rinse well and hang up. Drip-dry cottons may be wrung or spun for a short time, but then they will need to be ironed lightly. Do not boil drip-dry fabrics.

Silk Wash in warm water at 40°C, using a neutral soap or detergent. Knead and squeeze but avoid rubbing. Rinse several times, finishing with a cold water rinse. Silk articles may be wrung or spun dry, but light ones are better rolled in a towel to remove excess moisture, then allowed to dry for a short time before ironing. Multi-coloured silk that shows a tendency to run should be washed in cold salty water with a neutral soapless detergent. Rinse at once and spread out on a white cloth to dry quickly. Put a piece of white cloth inside to prevent the two sides touching while still wet.

Wool Knitted woollen garments are best washed by hand. Use water at 40°C and make a good lather with a neutral detergent, pure soap flakes or a product specially designed for washing wool. Wash by kneading and squeezing the fabric and avoid rubbing as this matts and shrinks the wool. Support the weight of the wool at all times to stop it stretching. Rinse thoroughly in water the same temperature as the washing water. Squeeze the water out gently – do not wring. Rolling woollens in a towel is a good way to remove some of the excess water without damaging the fibres.

Acetate and acrylic fibres (*Courtelle, Acrilan, Orlon, Tricel*) Wash frequently in water at not more than 40°C. Use soap or soapless detergent and rinse thoroughly. Remove moisture from a knitted garment by rolling it in a thick towel. Knitted jumpers can be put in a spin dryer for about a minute or until the machine reaches maximum speed. Dry flat and away from excess heat. Woven or jersey-knit fabrics should not be drip-dried. Excess moisture may be squeezed out and the garment dried flat. Acrylic fibres must be handled carefully during washing, drying and ironing as they tend to distort at high temperatures. They should never be bleached or boiled.

Nylon and polyester fibres (*Terylene, Dacron, Helanca, Enkalon*) Wash frequently to keep a good colour. For white nylon use water at 60°C or as hot as the hand can bear. Coloured nylon and polyester need lower temperatures – about 48°C – never more or permanent creases may form. Wash in a good lather of soap powder or detergent; rub to remove the dirt but avoid twisting the material. Rinse thoroughly and hang up to drip-dry. If spun, these fabrics will generally need ironing.

Viscose rayon fibres (*Vincel, Raycelon*) Handle with great care as rayon fibres lack the elasticity of other fabrics and the material becomes weaker when wet. Wash in hot water at 60°C with neutral soap or detergent, and avoid rubbing or twisting the fabric. Rinse several times in warm water and roll the garment in a towel before wringing it out. Be sure to support the weight of the material while it is wet. Rayon jersey should be dried flat or well supported on a double line. Never boil or bleach rayon or dry in direct heat.

WASH CODE	1 / 95	2 / 60	3 / 60	4 / 50	5 / 40	6 / 40	7 / 40	8 / 30	9 / 95
MACHINE WASHING	Hot to boil Maximum wash	Hot Maximum wash	Hot Medium wash	Hand-hot Medium wash	Warm Maximum wash	Warm Minimum wash	Warm Minimum wash	Cool Minimum wash	Very hot (95°C) to boil
AGITATION	Maximum	Maximum	Medium	Medium	Maximum	Minimum	Minimum	Minimum	Medium
RINSING, SPINNING, WRINGING	Spin or wring	Spin or wring	Cold rinse Short spin or drip-dry	Cold rinse Short spin or drip-dry	Spin or wring	Cold rinse Short spin Do not wring	Spin Do not hand wring	Cold rinse Short spin Do not wring	Cold Drip-dry
FABRIC	White cotton and linen fabrics without special finishes	Cotton linen or viscose without special finishes and colour-fast at 60°C	White nylon: white polyester/ cotton fabrics	Coloured nylon, polyester/ cotton; special finish cotton, viscose; acrylic cotton	Machine washable wool, cotton, linen, viscose; colours fast at 40°C but not at 60°C	Acrylics: acetate and triacetate; mixtures with wool; polyester/ wool blends	Wool, including blankets and mixtures of wool and cotton or viscose; silk	Silk and printed acetate fabrics with colours not fast at 40°C	Cottons with special finishes capable of being boiled but requiring drip-drying
BENEFITS	Ensures whiteness and stain removal	Keeps colour	Prolongs, whiteness, minimizes creasing	Keeps colour and finish, minimizes creasing	Keeps colour fastness	Keeps colour and shape, minimizes creasing	Keeps colour, size and handle (feel)	Prevents colour loss	Prolongs whiteness, retains special crease resistant finish

STARCHING

Some linen and cotton items respond well to starching which restores firmness to the fabric as well as encouraging a resistance to dirt. Light starching gives a crisp finish.

Boiling water starch Most commonly used for home laundering. Blend one tablespoonful (15ml) of starch with three tablespoonfuls (45ml) of cold water, then pour on boiling water, stirring well, until the starch clears. Dilute with cold water as directed on the packet, according to the degree of stiffness required.

After rinsing and wringing, immerse the articles in the solution, moving them around to ensure that the starch reaches all parts. Iron when evenly damp with a fairly hot iron, applying moderate pressure.

Plastic stiffener is sold in liquid form and should be diluted according to the manufacturer's instructions for the type of fabric and the degree of stiffness required. It gives a stiffness that may last through as many as twelve washes but produces a matt finish.

Spray-on starches These come in aerosols and are sprayed on to the fabric just before ironing. They are ideal for collars, cuffs and small items. As spray starch tends to leave a brown deposit on the base of the iron, use it last. Then unplug the iron, let it cool then clean the hotplate.

KEEPING IT WHITE

● Laundry borax added to soaking water helps loosen dirt from whites.

● Stubborn stains on whites may be removed by soaking overnight in milk.

● When boiling whites, a piece of lemon peel added to the water acts as a neutral bleach. (Not for automatics.)

● A few drops of washable blue ink added to the water helps to preserve the whiteness of nylon and lends a sparkle to white silk.

● Always wash whites separately.

KEEPING IT FAST

● Very brightly coloured clothes should be washed and dried inside out to prevent fading.

● Test clothes for colourfastness before washing by soaking a small area in hot water and squeezing it over the sink.

● Colourfastness can be improved with a little help. Try soaking black or red colours in salty water, green in alum, and blue in white vinegar. Brown, pink or grey items should be soaked in a mixture of salt and alum.

● Wash black clothes separately in case the colour runs.

● Try to avoid washing pale and dark or very bright colours together as the dyes may bleed.

KEEPING IT CLEAN

● Brush washing-up liquid or hair shampoo on to shirt collars to dissolve perspiration marks. Rub a paste made from white vinegar and bicarbonate of soda on to discoloured areas before washing to remove body oils.

● If fabrics are made from a mixture of fibres, choose a wash programme to suit the most delicate component.

● The most fragile fabrics, even lace or sheer tights and stockings, can be machine-washed. Prevent snagging by washing them inside a pillow case; tie up the end with a length of tape.

● White vinegar added to the final rinsing water acts as a fabric softener.

● Rubberized riding macs should be scrubbed on the outside using a soft brush and a mild detergent solution. Overlap the sections as you scrub so that it won't appear stripey when it dries. Never wash or wet the inside of the mac as it will destroy the waterproofing.

● Soak very dirty clothes for 30 mins before washing to help 'lift' the dirt.

DRYING

Never be tempted to dry wet clothes in an airing cupboard or in front of an open fire, both of which can be damaging. Always follow the care instructions on the garment's label, as explained in the chart on page 148.

Dry clothes as soon as you can after washing them: garments left damp for too long start to develop mildew. Never leave clothes until they're bone dry – it will be difficult to iron out the creases.

Electrically-operated tumble dryers have a rotating drum which allows clothes to move about freely in a current of heated air. Moist air is drawn off through a hose, usually outside. Most tumble driers have at least two heat settings – make sure you select the right one for the fabric. Never overload the machine or the clothes will get more crumpled and take longer to dry.

Don't put in permanently pleated items or anything with plastic fasteners that could melt.

Line drying is an economical and pleasant way to dry clothes if you have a garden or a yard, but is obviously not much use during prolonged wet or very cold weather.

Always peg clothes out by their strongest part, such as the waistband of a skirt. Turn white clothes inside out to dry in case there are specks of dirt in the air.

Don't peg woollen garments on a line or they'll stretch out of shape; dry them flat on a towel instead. To speed up the process, place a folded towel inside the body of the sweater and tubes of card inside the sleeves.

A drip-dry line or rack over the bath allows clothes to dry naturally, but it may take up to one or two days, depending on how warm your bathroom is.

IRON IT OUT

If you have a room where you can keep an ironing board permanently set up, giving a shirt a final press before wearing it will seem much less of a chore. The best ironing surface is one that has thick wadding (you could use worn-out blankets) underneath a removable cotton cover. Wash the cover as soon as it begins to look grubby and replace it when it starts getting threadbare. A strip of aluminium foil under your cover will speed up ironing by reflecting heat back through the underside of a garment. A sleeve board is the best way to iron sleeves without creases. Distilled water is best for steam ironing – or use water that's been boiled for 30 mins and left to cool.

If possible, iron clothes while they're still damp. Sprinkle dry clothes with water then roll them up and leave for 30 mins before ironing or, if you need to iron them immediately, use a fine-mist plant sprayer.

When ironing a garment made of mixed fibres, set the iron for the one needing the coolest temperature. If the iron starts to stick, take it off the fabric straight away – the iron is too hot. If the hotplate becomes coated with melted fibres, turn the heat to low and rub it on a pad of soft rags. You can also buy iron-cleaning sticks – but don't scratch the hotplate with anything abrasive.

It's a good idea to press skirts, jackets and trousers through a damp cloth, so the iron marks don't show. Some fabrics should be ironed on the wrong side to prevent shine.

Put dresses, skirts and blouses straight on to hangers. Avoid wearing ironed clothes immediately as they crease easily when newly pressed. Air all articles thoroughly – if you put ironed clothes away while they're still warm they may suffer from mildew.

 Cool iron – for acrylic, viscose, nylon, silk, acetate and polyester.

 Warm iron – use on polyester mixes, wool, wool and nylon mixes.

 **Hot iron** – for cotton and linen.

 **Do not iron** – it would harm the fabric.

DRYING OFF

● If your clothes get too dry to iron, put them in a cool dryer with a wet towel.

● Tumble-dry delicate garments (such as lace) inside a pillowcase to prevent them tangling with other articles.

● Dry tights quickly using a hair dryer.

● To prevent peg marks on a delicate top, thread a pair of tights through the sleeves and peg the ends to the line.

● Never leave white woollens to dry in the sunshine or they'll turn yellow.

UNDER PRESSURE

● Don't let a hot iron stray near nylon zips or plastic buttons – they will melt. Most irons have button grooves.

● Always steam velvet – don't iron it.

● Iron embroidery on the wrong side, preferably on top of a thick pad (such as a folded blanket).

● Remove scale by partially filling the iron with vinegar. Steam this away then fill with distilled water, and steam this away too. Or use a kettle descaler.

● To remove a sticky patch from the base of an iron, rub it backwards and forwards gently on a piece of paper, or half a lemon, sprinkled with salt.

● In general, iron along the length of a garment. But iron wool jersey with circular movements.

● Unstitched pleats are easier to iron if you tack them in before washing.

● Most dresses can be ironed round the board, or tackled as combined shirts and skirts, depending on the style.

● For a knife-edge crease, put drops of water along the edge, then iron through brown paper to draw the moisture out.

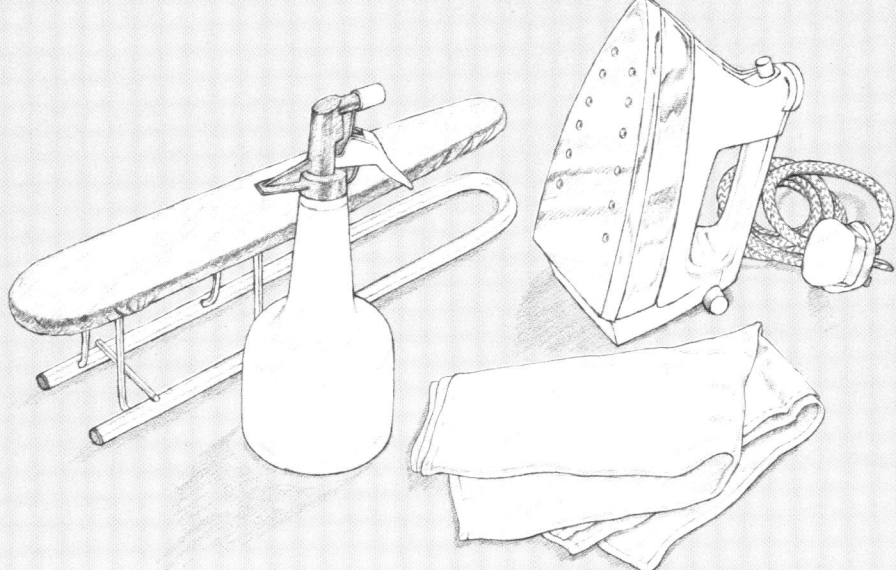

PRESSING SKIRTS

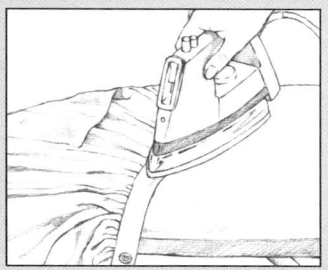

1 Start with the waistband of any skirt. Iron a straight or gored skirt flat, a pleated or gathered one by going round the board.

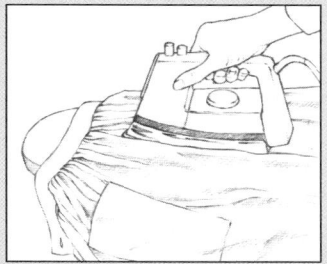

2 Push the point of the iron into gathers. It helps to hold gathers or tucks firmly in position with your other hand as you iron.

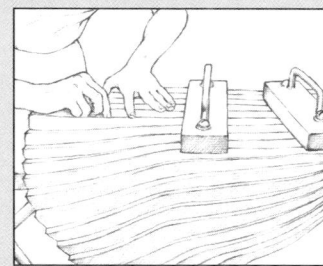

3 Use heavy weights to keep permanent pleats in while you press. You could use a strip of webbing with a weight at each end.

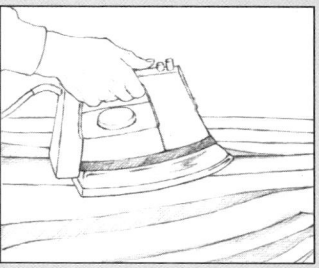

4 Starting from the zip, press each pleat on top and then, with the point of the iron, underneath.

PRESSING A SHIRT

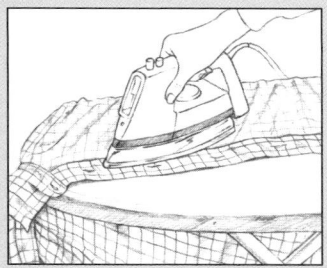

1 With the shirt inside out, dry off all the double-thickness areas such as the front tabs, seams, hem and yoke.

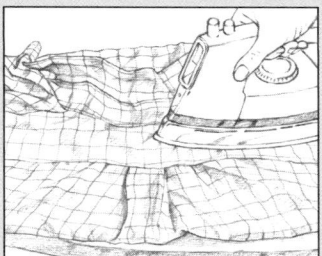

2 Right side out, fold shirt across the back about 5in (12cm) below the yoke. Keep this fold at the front edge of the board to iron the yoke.

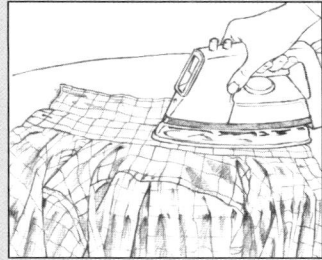

3 Press the collar, and the collar band, on the inside then the outside.

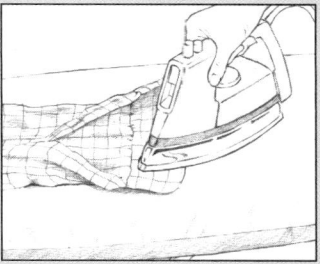

4 Iron the inside then the outside of the cuffs, stretching and smoothing any fullness towards the edge.

5 Fold sleeve along the underarm seam, lay it flat and iron to within ¼in (6mm) of the outer fold, easing into the fullness at the cuffs.

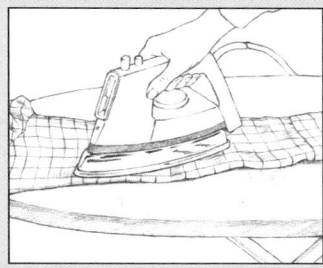

6 Turn and iron on the other side, then refold and press the unironed strip, carefully setting the pleat at the cuff edge.

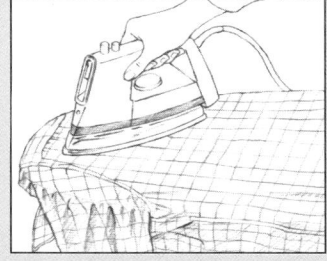

7 Iron the other sleeve. Lay the shirt over the board and iron the back.

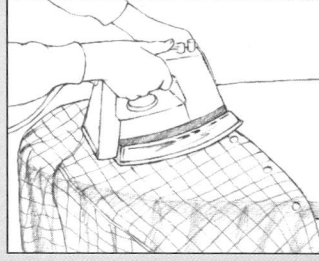

8 Press the two fronts, taking care round the buttons. Button the shirt and touch up any patchy areas or creases with the iron.

PRESSING TROUSERS

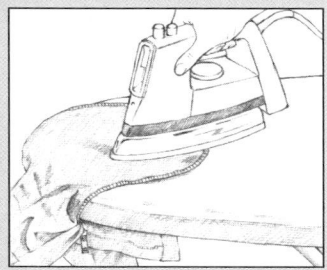

1 First dry off the inside pockets and make sure they lie flat.

2 Iron round the top of the trousers in 4 stages, being careful round the zip. Press each leg flat – but don't iron the side seams.

3 If the trousers require a centre-crease, hold by the ankles with the seams exactly opposite and shake. Put the folded legs flat on the board.

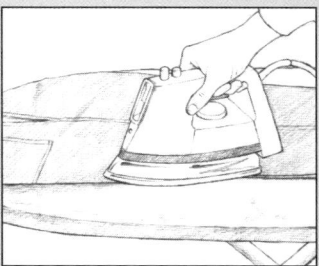

4 Iron firmly along both edges, pressing the crease in up to a front pleat and to back pockets – or to within 2in (5cm) of a waistband.

151

CARE AND REPAIR

The most important advice regarding stains is to act quickly. The longer a stain is in a fabric the more difficult it is to remove – and it may even damage the cloth.

Stains fall into two broad categories – water-soluble and greasy. It's no use attacking grease spots with water and a spirit-based cleaner is of no avail on a water-soluble stain.

Make sure you know the fabric of a garment before using any form of stain removal on it – and always check the label of a proprietary cleaner to see on what fabrics it can be used. (Acetates, for example, can't take vinegar, meths or commercial solvents; hydrogen peroxide must never be used on nylon or fabrics with a flameproof finish, nor ammonia on white wool or silk. And water damages viscose jersey and satin.) With a coloured fabric, first try out your remover on an unimportant part such as the inside of the hem.

Stains on garments marked 'dry clean only' and those made of delicate material should not be treated at home, apart from scraping off excess solids with a blunt knife or spatula. To be safe, always have unlabelled clothes, or those marked P or F, dry cleaned too. Never try to remove unidentifiable stains, or those more than a week old, yourself. If you know the stain tell a cleaner exactly what it is. And, if you have tried any form of stain removal yourself, inform them what products you used. If the stain isn't very obvious, use brightly coloured thread to mark it.

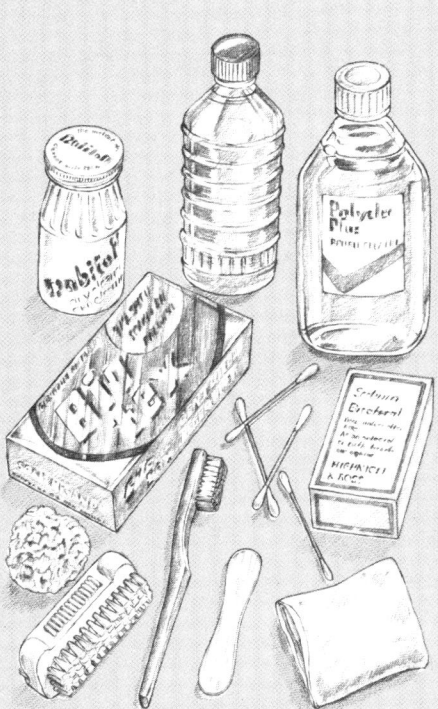

● Throw salt over highly coloured liquid stains, such as fruit, beetroot, red wine, blood, to absorb the colour.

● Shake talcum powder or cornflour on to grease-based stains to suspend them until you find the right solvent.

● *The colourfastness test* Lay the hem or seam on a piece of white cloth, apply the cleaning solvent, then place another piece of white cloth on top; press gently with a warm iron. If some colour comes off, don't attempt a home remedy.

● Always treat a stain on the wrong side of the fabric.

● Even gentle pressure may cause dull 'facing' on a dark silk garment. To camouflage, mix $\frac{1}{2}$pt (250ml) white spirit with 2 teaspoons (10ml) thin oil. Using a cloth pad, gently apply on wrong side to lay the fibres in the silk.

● Use a weak solution of any remover, repeating several times if necessary. Make a ring larger than the original stained area, and gradually work in.

● Use chemical solvents in a well-ventilated room and avoid inhaling the fumes. Wear rubber gloves.

● Don't throw white wine over red wine – you simply end up with two sets of stain to remove.

Keep a basic stain removal kit to hand, but make sure it's well out of the reach of children. It should contain:

Some clean, dry cloths – pieces of cotton sheeting are ideal.

Small sponges, for gentle dabbing.

Bicarbonate of soda, an alkaline, for neutralizing acid stains.

Washing soda, to dissolve greasy stains.

Methylated spirits (meths), for treating non-washable garments (except acetates).

Glycerine, to soften set stains.

White spirit, for paint stains.

Dilute ammonia (10%–15%) – but check for colourfastness and handle with care.

Dilute bleach (10%), for white cotton.

Hydrogen peroxide (20 vol) – mix 1 part to 6 parts water. Test for colourfastness.

Distilled white vinegar – mix 1 part to 5 parts water. An antidote to ammonia.

Borax, for neutralizing acid stains (it starts to bleach out colour after 15 mins).

Eucalyptus oil, for tar stains.

Proprietary grease solvents or dry cleaners, for grease stains.

Spray-on pre-wash treatments save rubbing and assist with make-up, grass and protein-based stains.

SIMPLE WATER-SOLUBLE STAINS

Sponge or dab the stain gently with a cloth under cold water. If it's persistant, use a solution of 1 teaspoon (5ml) washing-up liquid in 1 cup lukewarm water, or try bar soap and a soft nailbrush. Never use hot water – it may set the stain.

Beer ☐ Sponge with water then treat with distilled white vinegar solution. Rinse well, soak in biological detergent, then rinse again. If this doesn't work, use hydrogen peroxide solution, but test for colour-fastness first. On old stains, try meths. Finally, wash at highest temperature the fabric will take.

○ Distilled white vinegar solution, but not on acetates.

Contact adhesives ☐ Wash off with water *before* dry. Once dried, try meths.

○ Take straight to the dry cleaners.

Emulsion paint ☐ Scrape off excess, then flood with cold water. Rinse till all traces of paint have gone, then wash as usual. If marks remain, use a grease solvent.

○ Scrape off or blot up excess. Keep damp then take straight to dry cleaners.

Fruit stains ☐ Sprinkle with salt, then rinse in cold water till no more colour comes out. Stretch fabric over a bowl (tie string or a rubber band round to keep it in place), and pour over boiling water from a kettle, holding it as high as possible. Then wash at highest temperature for the fabric. If the stain is stubborn, soak in hydrogen peroxide solution. On wool, try distilled white vinegar solution.

○ Sponge gently, then clean.

Ink ☐ Rinse in cold water, under a running tap if possible. Treat from the back with liquid detergent, then rinse again. Treat remaining stain with equal quantities of lemon juice/ammonia/water.

○ Take straight to dry cleaners.

Latex adhesives ☐ Remove with a cloth soaked in water while still wet. Scrape off once dried.

Superglue This sticks in seconds, so act immediately – hold a pad soaked in water over the spot till it unsticks.

Wine ☐ Mop up excess liquid and cover red wine stain with salt. Rinse in cold water or sponge with warm water and soap, then rinse again. Squirt delicate fabrics with a soda syphon. Wash the garment as soon as possible.

○ With red wine, take straight to dry cleaners. Sprinkle white wine with talcum powder, leave a while then brush off. If stain remains, have it dry cleaned.

PROTEIN-BASED STAINS	STUBBORN STAINS	GREASE STAINS

PROTEIN-BASED STAINS

Scrape off any excess solids with a spatula or blunt knife.

○ Soak for several hours or overnight in cold water in which you've dissolved some biological detergent to break down the protein molecules. Don't soak wool or silk – wash them quickly in a solution of warm water and biological detergent.

Blood ⊔ Soak in strongly salted cold water. (If it has dried, use a stiff brush first.) Change the salted water several times until it's clear. Sponge any remaining stain with warm water and liquid soap – rinse again. Wash in biological detergent before stain dries.

○ Sponge gently with cold water and a few drops of ammonia. Rinse quickly and blot dry. Take to the dry cleaners.

Coffee ⊔ Soak in biological detergent. If it persists, treat with meths or hydrogen peroxide solution. Use dry cleaning solvent to remove residual grease, as well as on non-washable garments.

Curry ⊔ Soak in warm water, changing it until it runs clear, then rub in a solution of glycerine and warm water. Leave for 10 mins then rinse. Soak in biological detergent, then wash. White cotton and linens may need to be bleached.

○ Sponge from the back with a solution of borax and warm water. If the stain remains, take to the dry cleaners.

Perspiration ⊔ Soak in biological detergent. If stain persists, try warm soapy water with a few drops of ammonia in it. Rinse quickly. If the colour's affected, sponge with a distilled white vinegar solution (1 tbsp/15ml to ½pt/250ml warm water), then rinse.

○ Sponge with vinegar solution. If it affects the colour, dab with meths.

Tea ⊔ Soak in warm water and borax (1 tbsp/15ml to 1pt/500ml). Then soak in biological detergent and wash. Soften dried-on stains first with glycerine and warm water; if persistent, use meths.

Urine ⊔ Rinse well in cold water, then soak in biological detergent and wash. Soak old stains in hydrogen peroxide with a few drops of ammonia added.

○ Sponge with cold water, then with a distilled white vinegar solution (2 tsp/10ml to 2pts/1 litre water).

Vomit ⊔ Rinse under a cold tap then soak in biological detergent, adding a little disinfectant. Wash as usual. If marks remain, soak fabrics that can take it in hydrogen peroxide solution.

○ Sponge with a little ammonia in cold water or have dry cleaned.

STUBBORN STAINS

Immerse in dilute hydrogen peroxide, then wash thoroughly.

Chewing gum ⊔ Put the garment inside a plastic bag in the freezer for an hour to harden. The pieces should then break off easily. Loosen the traces by soaking in distilled white vinegar solution or rubbing with egg white before washing.

○ Freeze, remove pieces, then treat the traces with meths or white spirit.

Epoxy adhesives ⊔ Before they harden, use meths.

Grass ⊔ Work in neat washing-up liquid, sponge with warm water and liquid soap, and wash. Alternatively dab on a mixture of ammonia and soap or meths; rinse and wash.

○ Apply a paste of salt and cream of tartar mixed with a little water. Leave to dry, then brush out. If marks remain, use a proprietary stain remover or send to the dry cleaners.

Iron-mould or rust ⊔ Rub light stains with salt and lemon juice. Leave for 30 minutes then rinse well. Repeat if necessary. On heavier marks use a proprietary rust, iron-mould or dye remover, or an oxalic acid solution (1tsp/5ml to 2pts/1 litre water). But don't use these on silk or wool.

Mildew ⊔ Laundering may remove the marks; rub well with bar washing soap beforehand. Or soak white cotton and linen in a weak bleach solution (1tbsp/15ml to 2pts/1 litre water) with 1tsp/5ml distilled white vinegar added.

○ Dry clean.

Nail polish, clear adhesives ⊔ Blot up as much as possible, then treat from the back with amyl acetate, or a non-oily nail polish remover, then with white spirit. Follow up with meths.

○ Take straight to the dry cleaners.

Scorch marks ⊔ Wet fabric in cold water, then soak in a borax solution (2tsp/10ml to 2pts/1 litre of warm water). Wash as usual. Bleach white cotton or linen with a peroxide solution.

○ Sponge with borax solution, rinse and blot dry. Scorch marks cannot be completely removed from synthetics.

Tar, creosote ⊔ Scrape off excess, soften with glycerine then use eucalyptus oil, working from the back. Wash garment at hottest temperature it will take. A paint brush cleaner should shift any remaining stain.

○ After scraping and softening, try a dry cleaning solvent or dry clean.

GREASE STAINS

Use on butter, fat, cooking oil, salad dressing. With a fresh stain, scrape off excess and pat in talcum powder or cornflour. Brush off, then dab with a cloth pad soaked in carbon tetrachloride or a proprietary dry cleaner (don't use on rubber-backed items). Flush out with white spirit or a proprietary solvent, then wash at highest temperature the fabric will take. Soak delicate fabrics in a borax solution (1tbsp/15ml to 1pt/500ml warm water).

Carbon paper ⊔ Rub with neat washing-up liquid, then rinse well. If marks remain, try again, adding a few drops of ammonia to the soap.

○ Dab with meths or white spirit. On acetate or rayon use a suitable proprietary stain remover or take to the dry cleaners.

Ballpoint pen Don't attempt a home remedy. Take straight to the dry cleaners.

Felt tip pen ⊔ Dab on meths, then rub in liquid soap and wash.

○ Take straight to dry cleaners.

Gloss and oil paint ⊔ Flood with white spirit or brush cleaner, holding a clean pad under the stain. Then use a proprietary stain remover, and wash.

○ Take straight to the dry cleaners.

Lipstick ⊔ Rub glycerine or petroleum jelly into the stain to loosen it (use meths on nylon), then use a proprietary stain remover or grease solvent and wash.

○ Use a proprietary dry cleaner, or have garment professionally cleaned.

Make-up ⊔ Remove excess with a knife and pat in talcum powder. Treat light stains with warm water and detergent; soak heavier ones in ammonia solution (1tsp/5ml to 1pt/500ml lukewarm water). Wash.

○ Scrape off excess and pat in talcum powder. Then use an aerosol dry cleaning solvent or meths.

Mascara ⊔ Rub in neat washing-up liquid, then wash.

○ Treat with a dry cleaning fluid.

Newsprint Sponge with meths, then wash or have cleaned.

Shoe polish ⊔ Use white spirit or a proprietary paintbrush cleaner. Tackle small marks with an aerosol grease solvent. Wash in hot water and detergent, with a little ammonia added.

○ Spot-treat with aerosol dry cleaner.

⊔ washable garments
○ delicate or dry-clean-only garments

153

CHANGING COLOUR

Changing the colour of your clothes can give them a new lease of life. You can update a T-shirt or a simply-styled dress by dyeing it a more fashionable shade, or transform greying white undies.

It's important to know the fabric you're dyeing and to carry out the instructions to the letter. Some of the better-known dye companies will analyse a sample of fabric in their laboratories free of charge. You'll need to weigh the clothes before wetting them.

There are basically two sorts of chemical dye – cold water dyes which are suitable for all natural materials, and multi-purpose dyes, which are suitable for some synthetics too. Some companies also produce a liquid instant dye which is a hot water dye.

Both hot and cold water dyes can also be used in a washing machine if you're dyeing a lot of clothes. Dye no more than half the maximum load for best results. Wool must be dyed in hot water, so don't try to change the colour of a sweater that may shrink.

Chemical dyes are easy to use but it's fun to experiment with natural colourants such as coffee, tea, cochineal, madder, log-wood and turmeric. Weigh the clothes you want to dye and for each ounce (25g) of cloth use 1oz (25g) of leaves, berries or flowers or ½oz (12g) of spices, coffee or tea. If the water is hard, add softener or white vinegar. Put the dyestuff in a pan and barely cover with water. Soak leaves and berries overnight.

Bring the dyestuffs to a fast boil and boil for 30 mins, or until you obtain the desired colour. Measure the liquid concentrate and add enough water to make 2pts (1 litre) for each 1oz (25g) of cloth. In order for the dyes to take, you need to add a mordant. Immerse clean, wet articles for 30 mins, then rinse in successively cooler water.

● If your favourite white sweater has become grey, brighten it with Superwhite.

● Don't wash dyed clothes in biological powders, the colour will run.

● Always remove stains first otherwise the stain may not absorb the dye.

● Unless the garment to be dyed is white, the shade you'll end up with will be a blend of the original colour plus dye.

● To change a dark to a lighter colour, use a colour and stain remover first.

● If you dye your clothes in a washing machine, always clean it immediately afterwards by running it with hot water, detergent and 1 cup of bleach.

● Dyeing patterned material is a risky business, and only worth doing if you're overdyeing with the strongest colour in the pattern.

SHOE DYEING

Shoe paint is a simple and effective way to change the colour of your shoes. First clean or wash the shoes and use shoe trees or wads of newspaper to pad out the flex areas.

Go over the shoes thoroughly with pre-parer or conditioner, even if the shoes are brand new. This takes off the shine and enables the new colour to take properly. Then apply a coat of colour with the applicator provided, using even strokes. Two or three coats may be necessary to give a good finish, but let each coat dry thoroughly. As the fumes are pungent, it's a good idea to let the shoes dry out of doors. Finally, seal the colour and leave to dry.

Unlike dyeing clothes, shoe dye gives a true colour – it doesn't combine with the original shade to produce a mixture.

REPAIRING YOUR CLOTHES

A tear in a skirt, a ripped-off shirt button or a fallen dress hem aren't reasons to simply discard clothes. It's worth keeping a basic repair kit to hand (see page 146) and mastering some of the most common mending techniques in order to extend the life of your favourite clothes. 'Iron-on' mending tape can make lighter work of repairs and ready-made patches can be bought for jeans, as well as leather patches for jackets and thick sweaters.

Darning Match the threads as closely as possible to the colour and thickness of the fabric. It's not essential to use exactly the same fibre as the garment – a woollen sweater can be mended with wool/nylon thread which will give better wear. But threads of natural fibre are unsuitable for mending synthetic fabrics because they're not as strong and may shrink.

Use a needle that's long enough to pick up stitches along the whole length of the darn. An embroidery ring enables you to keep the cloth taut.

Patching Patches should be firm and nearly invisible. For a small patch, take material from the garment itself – the seam turning, hem allowance, inside pockets, facings or belt. Cut the patch large enough to cover the hole and any thin area around it and allow ½in (1cm) for turnings. Cut it exactly on the straight grain.

Zips For a temporary repair to a broken zip, take the slider down to the base. On the side that's come away, snip into the tape below the last visible tooth. Lift that tooth and slot it firmly into the top of the slider, then move the slider up to close the teeth. At the top of the remaining gap, work a strong bar tack into the tape across the teeth.

If you do need to replace a zip, make sure you buy one of the right weight and length.

Hems The weight of the fabric dictates which hemming stich you should use. Ordinary hem stitch (felling) is best on fine material such as cotton: sew from right to left (if you're right-handed), taking tiny stitches into the main material with a single thread. Hold the hem down with the thumb of your left hand, and keep the tension loose, otherwise it will pucker.

Use herringbone stitch on thicker material, working from left to right, again keeping the tension quite loose. It's easier if you put the garment on a table while you sew the hem, so the weight doesn't drag.

Always re-stitch a hem in the same way it was done originally. Thin fabrics are usually turned in and slip-hemmed, whereas on woollen and other thick cloths seam binding is first stitched to the raw edge, then hemmed to the garment, to avoid the bulk of a turning.

REPLACING A ZIP

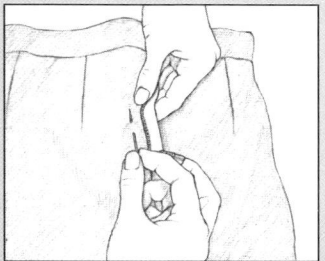

1 Having removed the old zip, pin the new one in place. Make sure the pull tag comes at the right level.

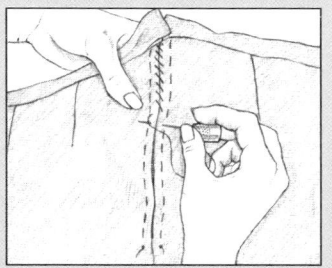

2 Tack the new zip in position, then oversew the edges of the opening together quite firmly, using diagonal stitches.

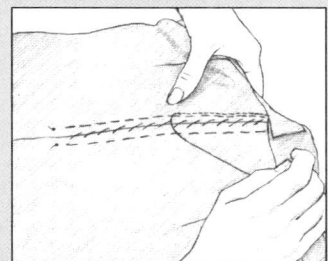

3 Unless you have a machine, backstitch firmly along both sides of the zip, following the original stitching lines.

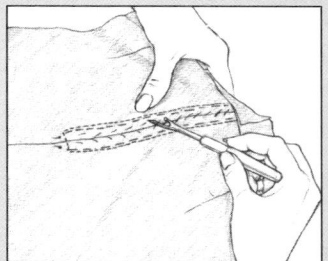

4 Hem down tape ends, then pull out all the oversewing and the tacking threads.

PATCHING

1 Take a ½in (1cm) turning all round the patch, then place it wrong side up on the wrong side of the garment; tack in position.

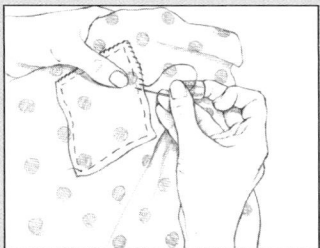

2 Hem all round, picking up only a thread or two of the garment. Make sure a stitch falls at each corner.

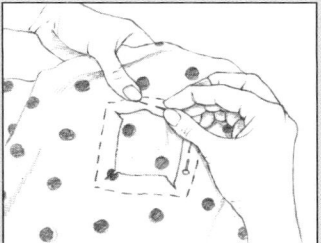

3 On the right side, trim the fabric inside the patch up to ⅜in (1.5cm) from the stitching. Clip ¼in (0.5cm) into each corner.

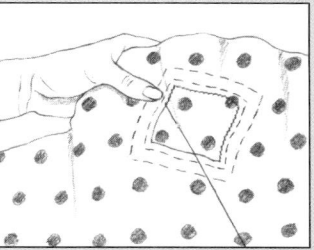

4 Fold under the raw edges and tack them in place. Press and fell, taking neat hemming stitches.

MENDING A TEAR

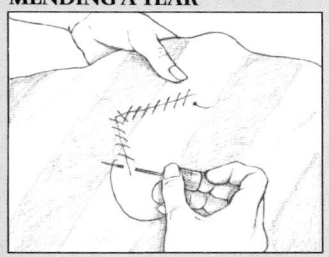

1 On a right-angled tear where the fabric's not too worn, tack the raw edges together by loosely oversewing on the right side.

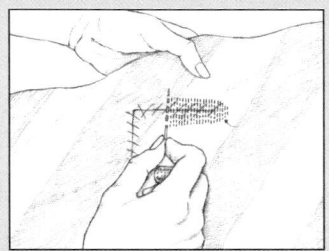

2 Work horizontal rows of close running stitch down from the top. Vary the length of the rows to make the darn less obvious.

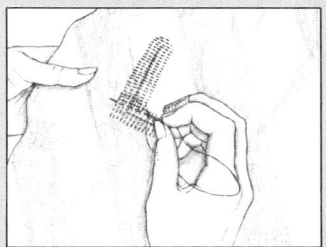

3 From the other end work rows of running stitch as far as the corner and a little beyond, so that the angle is strengthened by double stitching.

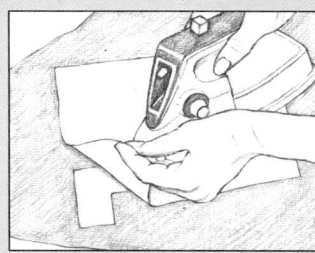

4 Where the material's worn thin, press an L-shaped piece of iron-on mending tape or interfacing to the wrong side of the garment.

RIPPED BUTTON AND TORN FABRIC

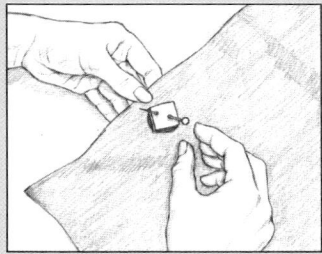

1 On an unlined garment, pin a piece of interfacing and a square of folded tape on the wrong side of the facing in the button position.

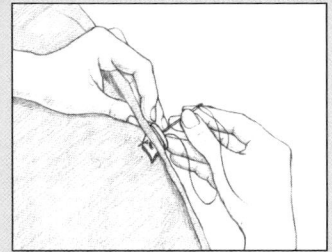

2 Settle the button in place on the right side of garment and sew it on, taking the thread through all layers. Remove the pin.

DARNING

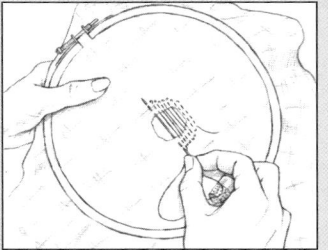

1 Weave stitches between groups of threads. Leave a small loop at the end of each strand to allow movement in the finished darn.

2 Weave in and out of the warp threads. Each strand should almost touch the next, so the hole will be completely filled.

Once you've taken your measurements carefully (as indicated on pages 12–13) you can use this chart to establish your most likely clothes size – and to ascertain where you're out of line with standard sizing. And if you're buying clothes or shoes abroad – or simply garments that have been made in another country – it's helpful to know how the sizes convert to those that are more familiar. So use these charts to get to know your body – its size and shape – better. It will give you more confidence at the clothes-buying stage.

A QUESTION OF PROPORTION

Whatever your size, there's an ideal set of body proportions. Very few women conform to it, of course, because nobody's perfect. But it can be helpful to know if, and where, you're seriously out of proportion so that you can choose clothes that camouflage, or minimize, the discrepancy.

Standing straight, with feet flat on the floor and arms by the side, the ideally proportioned body:
– breaks in half at the crotch
– the waist comes halfway between the armpit and crotch
– the elbow comes halfway down the arm and should line up with the waist
– the third knuckle reaches crotch height
– the knee comes halfway down the leg
– the nipple is 3in (7.6cm) below the armpit
– the shoulders are 1in (2.5cm) wider than the hips

CLOTHES SIZE GUIDE (in centimetres)						
British Size	8	10	12	14	16	18
American Size	6	8	10	12	14	16
European Size	36	38	40	42	44	46
Height	158	160	162	164	166	168
Nape to waist	39	39.5	40	40.5	41	41.5
Knee length	94	95.5	97	98.5	100	101.5
Body rise	25.8–26	26.3–26.5	26.8–27	27.3–27.5	27.8–28	28.3–28.5
Outside leg	99.4	100.7	102	103.3	104.6	105.9
Chest	73–75	77–79	81–83	85–87	89–91	93–95
Bust	78–80	82–84	86–88	90–92	94–96	98–100
Waist	57–59	61–63	65–67	69–71	73–75	77–79
Hips	84–86	88–90	92–94	96–98	100–102	104–106
Half across back	15.5–15.8	16–16.3	16.5–16.8	17–17.3	17.5–17.8	18–18.3
Shoulder	11.5–11.6	11.7–11.8	11.9–12	12.1–12.2	12.3–12.4	12.5–12.6
Outer arm length	70.7–71	71.7–72	72.7–73	73.7–74	74.7–75	75.7–76
Under arm length	41.4–41.6	41.6–41.8	41.8–42	42–42.2	42.2–42.4	42.4–42.6
Upper arm	23.2–24	24.6–25.4	26–26.8	27.4–28.2	28.8–29.9	30.2–31
Wrist	13.8–14.2	14.4–14.8	15–15.4	15.6–16	16.2–16.6	16.8–17.2
Thigh	51–52	53–54	55–56	57–58	59–60	61–62
Knee	32.5–33	33.5–34	34.5–35	35.5–36	36.5–37	37.5–38
Ankle	29.5–30	30.5–31	31.5–32	32.5–33	33.5–34	34.5–35

SHOE SIZE GUIDE					
British Size	3	4	5	6	7
American Size	4½	5½	6½	7½	8½
European Size	36	37	38	39	40

Use this scale to convert from metric into imperial measurements – or vice versa.

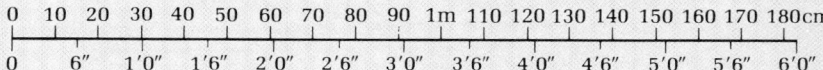

AUTHOR'S ACKNOWLEDGEMENTS
In everyone's career there are people who
stand out as the ones who really helped.
There are two such in mine: two women
who put their faith and trust in me and,
cliché though it may sound, taught me
everything I know about the business.
Firstly, there is June McCallum, former
fashion editor of *Good Housekeeping* (UK),
and now editor of *Vogue* (Australia), whose
unerring good taste still influences my
fashion styling today. And latterly,
Katherine Hadley, woman's editor of the
Daily Express, who showed me how to face
a typewriter without too much fear – but
with just enough.

More specifically there are a tremendous
number of people who have helped me to
research and write this book. Too many to
be listed, but for the record here are some
individuals who were so generous with
their time and knowledge that I simply
could not conclude the book without
thanking them by name. Nat Bury of the
London College of Fashion, Betty Williams
of Berlei, Sue Loder and Jo St Clair of
Triumph, David Shilling, John Boyd, Philip
Somerville, Susie Gold of Wardrobe, Debbie
Rudd of Arena, Gill Hewitt of Options at
Austin Reed, Nina Hirst of Fabric Forecast,
Kay Cornelius of The Colour Company,
Audrey Levy, colour consultant, Babette
Monteil, wardrobe consultant, Jean
Cooper, physiotherapist, Jean King of
Lillywhites, fashion stylist, Rebecca Tyrell
and Jackie Modlinger, Keri Beak and
Audrey Sparks of the *Daily Express*.

I would also like to thank Rosemary
Mills, beauty editor of *Company* magazine,
who wrote the beauty pages so expertly and
Sue Locke, whose care and repair
knowledge was totally invaluable. I have
learnt a lot from both these sections – I hope
that you will too.

SUPPLIERS' CREDITS

102–3 Santos watch, *Cartier*; crystal beads, earclips, *Fenwicks*; silk separates, *Lumière*; lambswool cardigan, *The Scotch House*; slippers, *Whistles*. 114–15 Textured wool separates, *I Blues*; shoes, *Hobbs*; furry coat, *Georges Rech*. 116–17 Pleated skirt, *Roland Klein*; sweater dress, *Stefanel*. 118–19 Shoes, *Hobbs*; print separates, *Gay Ironmonger*; shirtdress, *Maxfield Parrish*. 122–3 Tuxedo, *Cerruti*; dress and coat, *Erreuno*; knitted suit, *Joseph Tricot*. 126 Dress, *Cornucopia*. 128–9 Lace collar and jabot, *Eve's Lace, Stall X6, Antiquarius*; lace gloves, shoes, fan, *Persiflage, Stall Y8, Antiquarius*; scarves and jewellery, *Dickens and Jones*; cream trousers, *Fenn, Wright and Manson*; hat, *Fenwicks*; sandals, *Hobbs*; cotton and lace blouse and skirt, lace stole, trimming, modesty bolero, *Lunn Antiques*; belt, *Mulberry*; red suede jacket, *Maxfield Parrish*; silver and onyx bracelet, paste cross, paste and metal tiara, *The Purple Shop*. 132–3 Earrings, *Dinny Hall*; clothes, *Issey Miyake*. 136–7 Crocodile skin belt with solid silver buckle, *Browns*; Vendôme 'Santos' wristwatch, tank watch with pigskin strap, diamond triple bangle, gilt-rimmed sunglasses, diamond, emerald and gold suite, *Cartier*; white silk hair bow, *Chanel*; spotty gloves, *Fenwicks*; strawberry print silk scarf, gold knot ring and bangle, gold chain and crocodile belt with GG buckle, *Gucci*; kid gloves, *Harvey Nichols*; 'Kelly' bag, *Hermès*; duck-handled umbrella, spotty silk scarf, *Liberty*; reptile clutch bag, *Russell & Bromley*; LV clutch bag, *Louis Vuitton*; gold Rolex watch, *Watches of Switzerland*. 138–9 Rubber knot earclips and bangles, *Accessoire*; Mickey Mouse watch, *Clerkenwell Green*; beads, *Corocraft*; geometric bangles, *Detail*; rubber action watch, plastic paperchain necklace and bracelet, *Fenwicks*; splash print belt and shell earrings, *Harvey Nichols*; robot watch, leather bow belt, *Joseph*; chiffon scarf, *Kenzo*; anchor earrings, *Liberty*; hair pegs, bow hairclips, tiny shoulder bag and netting scarf, *Miss Selfridge*; splash print scarf, *Way In* at *Harrods*. Inset left, peach and white scarves, orange T-shirt, *Fenwicks*; glass necklace, *Michaela Frey*; blue and white cotton scarf, *Whistles*. Inset right, 'Love' socks, *Chelsea Girl*; paisley scarf, *Fenwick's*; earclips, *Michaela Frey*; orange and white scarf and dungarees, blue rubber belt, *Pacific*; telephone strap key ring, *Miss Selfridge*; sunglasses, *Whistles*. 140–41 Ring pull earclips, *Accessoire*; steel bracelet and star necklace, *Butler & Wilson*; black and gold belt, *Stephen Collins*; black chain, *Corocraft*; clear-framed mirror spectacles and upswept-side spectacles, *Cutler & Gross*; jet and diamanté earrings, wide gilt bangles, *Detail*; black 'Rayban' wraparound sunglasses, animal print scarf and pouch, *Fenwicks*; rubber and paste earrings, black plastic and paste bracelet, diamanté hoops, *Harvey Nichols*; zebra print belt, *Galleries Lafayettes*; glass and steel earclips, *Liberty*; black rubber matting shopping bag, *Pink Soda*; rhinestone necklace, *Miss Selfridge*. 142–3 Ethnic scarf, mother of pearl necklace, palm leaves necklace, *Accessoire*; pewter earclips, *Corocraft*; leather necklace, *Detail*; big marble bangle, *Harvey Nichols*; stretchy string belt, *Daniel Hechter*; terracotta scarf and hessian bag, *Kenzo*; Indian, multi-strand necklace, Celtic silver choker, triple and single armlets, ring, semi-precious stone brooch, bracelet and buckle, bead necklace with large gold disc, wooden bangles, brass stud earclips, *Liberty*; oval cracked earclips, cracked bangle, cracked and gilt necklace, punched metal and stone necklace and stone bangle, *Pellini*; string choker with metal bands, *Pink Soda*. 144–5 Revolver cufflinks, medal, *Detail*; watch on rubber strap, *Ferrari*; tortoiseshell-framed glasses, *Harvey Nichols*; spot tie and silk cufflinks, *Hilditch & Key*; stripe tie, cashmere scarf, floral bow tie, driving gloves, shirt, evening scarf, stripe cufflinks, *Liberty*; armbands, briefcase, *Mulberry*; wing collar, *New & Lingwood*; man's wristwatch, *Omega*; man's diving watch, *Seiko*; antique watch, *Vacheron Constantin*.

PICTURE CREDITS

l = left; *r* = right; *t* = top; *b* = bottom

8–9 David Hamilton/The Image Bank; 10*l Woman's Own*/Syndication International; 10*r Grazia*/Transworld; 11 Carrara/*Elle*/Transworld; 13 *Honey*/Syndication International; 14–15 Peter Rauter/hair by Robert at Schumi; 16–17 Peter Rauter; 18*t* Brian Aris/Duncan Paul Associates; 18*b* Alistair Morrison/*Fitness*; 19*tl* Brian Aris/Duncan Paul Associates; 19*tr* Topham Picture Library; 19*b Woman's Own*; 20–1 Illustration by Gina Toone; 22 *Options*/Syndication International; 23 *Honey*/Syndication International; 25 Yavel/*Elle*/Transworld; 26–7 Tapie/*Elle*/Transworld; 28 Perry Ogden/Laura Ashley; 28–9 John Swanell/Harvey Nichols; 29 J.A.P.; 30 Fabrizio Ferre/*Harpers & Queen*/The National Magazine Co; 31 Tony McGee/*Company*/The National Magazine Co; 32 Elaine Chaloner; 33 Dee Dawson; 34 Victor Yuan; 34–5 Elia/*Elle*/Transworld; 37 Triumph International/Butler Dennis Garland & Partners Ltd; 38*l* Molton Brown; 38*r* Toni & Guy; 39*l* Hanson/*Elle*/Transworld; 39*r* Stuart MacLeod/*Good Housekeeping*/The National Magazine Co; 40 Toni & Guy; 40–1 Bill King; 41 Hanson/*Elle*/Transworld; 42 Wayne Günther; 43 Holz/*Elle*/Transworld; 44*t* Polo Ralph Lauren; 44*b* Keystone Press Agency; 45 Marc Hispard/*Harpers & Queen*/The National Magazine Co; 46–7 Polo Ralph Lauren; 47 Hanson/*Elle*/Transworld; 48 Nick Briggs; 49 Hauss/*Elle*/Transworld; 50*t* Tony McGee/*Company*/The National Magazine Co; 50*b Grazia*/Transworld; 51 Tony McGee/*Company*/The National Magazine Co; 52 *Honey*/Syndication International; 53 Michael Doster/Escada; 54 Polo Ralph Lauren; 54–5 Hypard/*Elle*/Transworld; 56–7 Mondi; 59 *Honey*/Syndication International; 61 Tapie/*Elle*/Transworld; 62 Tony McGee/*Harpers & Queen* promotion for David Hicks/The National Magazine Co; 63 *Options*/Syndication International; 64*l* Silverstein/*Elle*/Transworld; 64*r* Elia/*Elle*/Transworld; 65 B. Hansen/The Image Bank; 66–7 J. de Sauversac/The Image Bank; 68–9 Rose/*Elle*/Transworld; 69 John Bishop/Warehouse Group PLC; 70*t Grazia*/Transworld; 70*b* John Bishop/Warehouse Group PLC; 70–1 Tony McGee/Mulberry Co; 72 Silverstein/*Elle*/Transworld; 73 Bensimon/*Elle*/Transworld; 74*l* Duc/*Elle*/Transworld; 74*r* Sandra Lousada/*Harpers & Queen* promotion for Mulberry Co/The National Magazine Co; 75 Mario Testino/*Harpers & Queen*/The National Magazine Co; 76 Jaeger; 77 *Woman's Journal*/Syndication International; 78*l* Martin Brading/Miss Selfridge; 78*r Grazia*/Transworld; 79 Wallis Fashion Group Ltd; 80*t Grazia*/Transworld; 80*b* Perry Ogden/Next; 81 Pamela Hanson/*Harpers & Queen*/The National Magazine Co; 82 The Sunday Times; 83 Over 21; 84–5 Hispard/*Elle*/Transworld; 86 John Bishop/Warehouse Group PLC; 87 Leo Mason; 88 Mondi; 89 *Donna Sport*/Transworld; 90 Trautwein/*100 Cose*/Transworld; 90–1 Pindisports Ltd; 91 Lillywhites Ltd; 92 Caminata/*Donna*/Transworld; 93*l* Richard Steedman/The Image Bank; 93*r* Lange/*Elle*/Transworld; 94*t* Mungai/*Bella*/Transworld; 94*b* Berton/*Parents*/Transworld; 95 *Biba*/Transworld; 96–7 Frontini/*Linea Italiana*/Transworld; 98*t* D. Issermann/Sygma/The John Hillelson Agency; 98*b* Jouvelle/*Elle*/Transworld; 99*t* Silverstein/*Elle*/Transworld; 99*b* Graham Hughes/*Company*/The National Magazine Co; 100 Silverstein/*Elle*/Transworld; 101*t* Eric Blum; 101*b* Rau/*Elle*/Transworld; 102*l* Bensimon/*Elle*/Transworld; 102*r* Mondi; 103*l* Wickrath/*Linea Italiana*/Transworld; 103*r* Nick Briggs; 105 Fabrizio Ferre/*Harpers & Queen*/The National Magazine Co; 106 *Bella*/Transworld; 107 *Grazia*/Transworld; 108 Bensimon/*Elle*/Transworld; 109 Carrara/*Elle*/Transworld; 110 Chanel Ltd; 110–11 Paul Lange/*Harpers & Queen*/The National Magazine Co; 111 Serge Krouglikoff; 112*l Woman's Journal*/Syndication International; 112*r* Carrara/*Elle*/Transworld; 113 Bruno Juminer/*Harpers & Queen*/The National Magazine Co; 114–15 Mondi; 116 *Honey*/Syndication International; 118 Nick Briggs; 119 Meroz/*Linea Italiana*/Transworld; 121*l* Fouli/*Elle*/Transworld; 121*r Grazia*/Transworld; 123 Mike Yavel/Maxmara; 124 Feurer/*Elle*/Transworld; 125 Neil Kirk/*You Magazine*; 127 Neil Kirk/*Company*/The National Magazine Co; 128 Peter Rauter; 129 *Grazia*/Transworld; 130 Hanson/*Elle*/Transworld; 131 Liberty; 132 Tapie/*Elle*/Transworld; 133*l* Rose/*Elle*/Transworld; 133*r* Nick Briggs; 134–5 Carrara/*Elle*/Transworld; 136–7 Charlie Stebbings; 137*inset* Keystone Press Agency; 138–9 Charlie Stebbings; 138–9*insets* Nick Briggs; 140–1 Charlie Stebbings; 140*inset* Neil Kirk/*You Magazine*; 141*inset* Chanel Ltd; 142–3 Charlie Stebbings; 143*inset* Alexon; 144–5 Charlie Stebbings; 144*inset* Andrew MacPherson/*Harpers & Queen*/The National Magazine Co; 145*inset* Victor Yuan.

The Mail on Sunday, quotes by V. Principal, 19.

Artwork/Retouching

Graham Bingham
Roy Flooks
Brian Mayor